THE OPEN MEDIA PAMPHLET SERIES

THE OPEN MEDIA PAMPHLET SERIES

The Progessive Guide to ALTERNATIVE MEDIA AND ACTIVISM

PROJECT CENSORED

Series editors Greg Ruggiero and Stuart Sahulka

SEVEN STORIES PRESS / New York

A Seven Stories Press First Edition,
published in association with Open Media.

Open Media Pamphlet Series editors,
Greg Ruggiero and Stuart Sahulka.

Library of Congress Cataloging-in-Publication Data

The progressive guide to alternative media and activism.
p.   cm. -(The Open Media Pamphlet Series: #8)
ISBN 1-888363-84-3 (pbk.)
1. Mass media-Directories. 2. Underground press-Directories.
I. Project
Censores (U.S.) II. Series: Open media pamphlet series; 8.
P88.8.P76 1998
302.23'025-dc21   98-30137
                                          CIP

Book design by Cindy LaBreacht

9 8 7 6 5 4 3 2 1

ACKNOWLEDGMENTS

Project Censored would like to thank the 800 plus alternative press organizations and media activists groups listed in this resource guide for their cooperation and support of this effort. It is your dedication to freedom of the press and the truth in news that give us the optimism to believe that a democratic news and information system in the United States and the world in not just a dream but a real possibility.

Numerous students and staff with Project Censored worked on this resource guide: special recognition goes to research team leaders to Katie Simms and Alix Jestron along with student researchers Ken Downing, Suzanne Murphy, Yvette Tannenbaum, Cathy Hickinbotham, Janice Garcia, and Chantille Hickman. Trish Boretta, Project Censored's intern coordinator, spent many hours assisting the research efforts and coordinating the responses. Scott Fraizer and Michael Smith are actively working on the next phase of this resource guide by linking Project Censored's web site a www.sonoma.edu/projectcensored/ to all the alternative press organizations listed.

Sonoma State University's administration, faculty and staff have made this effort possible with technical assistance, library support, office space, and numerous other in-kind donations. Thank you one and all.

Peter Phillips
Director, Project Censored

Freeing the Media

BY PETER PHILLIPS

Twenty-two years ago there where approximately fifty media corporations dominating U.S. news services. Today there are less than a dozen. The Federal Communications Commissions used to limit television and radio station ownership. Since the passage or the Telecommunications Act in 1996, a single corporation may now own radio, television, book publishing, newspapers, and Internet services all in the same market area and up to a one third market share nationally. This means that the dozen major media corporations that own most of our news systems today could further consolidate to 3 or 4 corporations in the next decade.

Mainstream media is in a gold rush of acquisitions and mergers including: Time Warner's merger with CNN, ABC being taken over by Disney, and Westinghouse (CBS) buying up Infinity Radio Group. Over one-third of all the radio stations in the United states have sold within the last 18 months. This is happening in the newspaper industry as well. Gannett, and Knight-Ridder have taken the lead in ownership of newspaper chains, together holding close to 200 metropolitan news publications.

The U.S. media has lost its diversity and its ability to present different points of view. Instead there is a homogeneity of news stories, and major media tends to look increasingly alike. Entertainment and fear and have become our principal news stories in the U.S. press and broadcast media. The American public watches celebrity news, infomercials, titillation, and sex as entertainment. Crime reports, stories of the under-class, immigrants, and welfare cheats create fear and loathing. Crime reporting has tripled in this decade while the actual rate of crime has declined. The media in the U.S. has created, to use Neil Postman's words, the "best entertained, least informed society in the world". Americans are increasingly more ignorant about international affairs, and alienated from their own social issues.

Last year researchers at Project Censored looked up the names of the people who serve on the boards of directors of the eleven media companies dominating the U.S. market. A total of 155 people sit on these boards. They include men like:

Frank Carllucci, who sits on Westinghouse's (CBS) board, was former deputy director of the CIA, and later Secretary of Defense under President Bush;

Andrew Sigler, who serves on GE's (NBC) board, also sits on the board of directors of Chemical Bank, Bristol Meyers Squibs, Allied Signal, Champion International and Chase Manhattan Bank; or

Douglas Warner III, who sits on GE's (NBC) board, also sits on the board of directors of Bechtel Group, Anheuser-Busch, and is the CEO of J.P. Morgan Company.

The 155 media elite are mostly individuals who inherited wealth, were educated in private preparatory schools and ivy league universities, and whose main social interactions occur at the Knickerbockers Club in New York, Bohemian Grove in California or the Piedmont Driving Range in Atlanta. They represent private wealth, private education, private clubs, conservative politics and they control the way most Americans get their information and news.

The top 11 media corporations in the U.S. form a solid grid of overlapping interests and affiliations. The 155 directors of these 11 media corporations sit on the boards of directors of 144 of the Fortune 1000 corporations and interlock with each other through shared directorships in other firms some 36 times.

NBC, Fox News, and Time Warner each has a board member who sits as a director on tobacco producer Phil Morris's board. CBS (Westinghouse) shares directorships on Fortune 1000 boards with the *Washington Post*, Time-Warner, NBC (GE), Gannett, Viacom and the Times Mirror Corporation (L.A. Times).

Little wonder that the U.S. news is so biased against democratic liberation struggles all over the world and so favorable to multi-national capital flow, International Monetary Fund polities, GATT, MAI, NAFTA, and all the other neoliberal economic policies that favor the free flow of international capital and wealth acquisition. Democracy, to the media elite, means freedom to economically exploit, freedom to move money anywhere in the world, and freedom to present their own ideological messages.

The U.S. media ignores fundamental issues like:

➤ Who loses in the process of economic growth and wealth accumulation?

➤ What about the one billion people in the world who are seen as surplus labor and un-needed in the international market place?

➤ What about the global issues of environmental sustainability and the using up of our unrenewable natural resources?

These are the questions of a socio-environmental apocalypse. The collapse of a market system defined by exponentially growing levels of wealth concentration and elite consumption is inevitable. Free market capitalism is creating an unaccountable system of corruption and waste that generates wretchedness for billions of people. All the indicators are that wealth and resources do not trickle down, but rather becomes increasingly concentrated in the hands of the elites in the nation states of the first world and their senior and junior partners around the globe.

What hope have we? What direction can resistance take? I believe that we are not going to meaningfully reform the international global media system, especially in the United States. Media wealth is too concentrated, too solidified, and too integrated into the corporate-government elite to make genuine democratization of the existing system possible.

We can, however, look to ourselves for the direction we must go. In the past several years there have been increased grassroots organizing around issues of media and democracy; from *Z* magazine's annual Z Media Institute and the formation of groups like the Grassroots News Network the Direct Action Media Network, and the New York Free Media Alliance, to the two Cultural Environment Movement conventions and two Media and Democracy Congresses.

"Media and Democracy" has become a grass roots movement based on a shared vision of building alternative news and information systems independent from corporate influence. Hundreds of pirate radio stations, many now under attack by the FCC have sprung up all over the U.S. offering a diversity of programs. Fairness and Accuracy in Reporting, Independent Media Institute, and numerous First Amendment groups, Internet newsletters, and news magazines are active all over the United States. Progressive media networks exist in L.A., Chicago, Denver, San Francisco, Houston, New York, and Seattle. TV producers from Free Speech TV, People's Video, Globalvision, Deep Dish, and Paper Tiger TV are being joined by small progressive shoe-string-budget cable show producers all over the country: People like school teacher John Morearty in Stockton California, who for five years has been doing a weekly hour long progressive TV show aired in his local community. The Pacific Radio network has been joined with Hightower Radio and United Broadcasting, and over 100 alternative newsweeklys are published in almost every major metropolitan area in the U.S. Two video producers, Beth Sanders and Randy Baker made the film "Fear and Favor in the Newsroom" that describes the consequences of media monopoly. This film is being shown at activist meetings all over the country.

Alternative/independent media sources in the U.S. are still small, often territorially competitive and under-financed. Yet they offer a hope for the future.

Academics, progressives and leftists have been rightly criticized for being intellectually elitist and condescending. Michael Moore criticized the Media and Democracy Congress in New York for its failure to incorporate working class people into its agenda. Moore asks, "where is the woman at Sears who sells blouses by day and then wait-resses at Denny's from 8:00 P.M. to Midnight"?

This is a criticism that we cannot ignore! The 60% of the population who are blue and white collar workers surviving paycheck to paycheck are alive and well. Yet they are con-fused by a media system that can't or won't explain why the value of their paychecks have declined for 25 years, why health care costs are so high, why housing is unafford-able, and their taxes keep increasing. How can we, as we build real alternatives to the commercial media system, create real access and participation from all sectors of our communities?

Major media have led working people towards racial hatred, immigrant bashing, and attacks on welfare. People are fearful of the homeless because they fear homelessness themselves. They blame and attack the victims of corpo-rate greed. They pay high tuition to send their children to state universities. These students often end up back home after graduation with huge student loan debts and few professional prospects for employment. Most working people are politically alienated and more than half no longer vote.

Yet, working people have strong core values that honor meaningful work, democratic process, equal opportunity, freedom of expression, due process, and systemic fairness. Several times over the past 100 years working people have joined with progressives, forming social movements that changed the United States. The Progressive Movement 100 years ago challenged the Robber Barons and corporate wealth concentration and instituted income tax on the rich, an 8 hour work day, the rights of governmental recall, and citizen proposition. The Suffrage movement gave women the right to vote. The Labor Movement in the 1930s forced a New Deal that allowed unionism, national social welfare, old age pensions, and national public health. The Civil Rights Movement broke the back of racial segregation and the Peace Movement challenged the illegal war in Vietnam. The Environmental Movement, the American Indian Movement, and the Women's Movement have all made needed changes in society. Each of these movements depended on thousands of working people, who contributed, marched and in many cases died for their beliefs.

We must, and we can reawaken the values of the working people in order to mobilize against the socio-environmental apocalypse being ignored by corporations and the media they own and control. A free flow of ideas will only happen outside of corporate media, outside of the government-corporate spin doctors.

An alternative/independent press can be a key element in a social movement that empowers working people in the U.S. to take control of their government-corporate power structures for their own betterment and the betterment of the world. "Free the Media" can become a real rallying cry that will allow the emergence of what the new democratized AFL-CIO calls "Common Sense Economics" an economics that unmasks corporate wealth exploitation for the betterment of working people worldwide.

Can we strengthen alternative/independent news systems in the United States? I believe we can by sharing news stories, Internet connections, joint publicity/outreach plans, and by addressing the important socio-economic, environmental, gender and racial issues in the U.S. and in the world.

For people in the U.S. this means building and supporting alternative news and information systems, and becoming local activists with global awareness. For those outside the U.S. it means sharing viewpoints, news stories, information with the alternative press in the U.S., and helping reeducate working people to our shared global problems.

Project Censored offers this pamphlet as a small effort in a major battle to free our news and information systems in the United States. To find out more about the Free Media Movement contact us at Censored@sonoma.edu. or by mail:

Project Censored's Resource Guide Team
Sonoma State University
1801 East Cotati Ave.
Rohnert Park, CA 94928.

NATIONAL ALTERNATIVE PUBLICATIONS

14850 MAGAZINE
95 Brown Road, Suite 210
Ithaca, NY 14850
(607) 257-1831
Fax: (607) 257-1873
pci@14850.com
http://www.14850.com

A little of everything, from humor to local interest.

ABILITIES
489 College St. Suite 501
Toronto, ON MG6 1A5
Canada
(416) 923-1885
Fax: (416) 923-9829
able@interlog.com
http://www.enablelink.org

Published by the Canadian Abilities Foundation, this magazine is for people with disabilities, their families, and friends.

ABORIGINAL VOICES
116 Spandina Ave., Suite 201
Toronto, ON M5V 2K6
Canada
(800) 324-6067
or (416) 703-4577
Fax: (416) 703-4581
abvoices@inforamp.net
http://www.cac.mall.com

Focuses on indigenous art, literature, culture, media and entertainment.

ABOUT...TIME
MAGAZINE
283 Genesee St.
Rochester, NY 14611
(716) 235-7150
atmag@abouttime.com
www.abouttimemag.com

This monthly focuses on issues of international, national and regional importance reflecting the African-American experience.

ABYA YALA NEWS:
Journal of the South and MesoAmerican Indian Rights Center
P.O. Box 28703
Oakland, CA 94604
(510) 834-4263
Fax: (510) 834-426
abyayala@nativeweb.org
http://www.nativeweb.org/
    abyayala

Deals with environmental and human rights issues with focus on indigenous people in Latin America and elsewhere.

ADBUSTERS:
A Magazine of Media and Environmental Strategies
1243 West Seventh Ave.
Vancouver, BC V6H 1B7
Canada
(604) 736-9401
Fax: (604) 737-6021

adbusters@adbusters.org
http://www.adbusters.org/
  main/index.html

Strategies for fighting mind
pollution from commercial-
ism and advertising.

ADVOCATE, THE
6922 Hollywood Blvd.
Ste 1000
Los Angeles, CA 90028
(213) 871-1225
Fax: (213) 467-6805
newsroom@advocate.com
www.advocate.com

Leading national gay and
lesbian news magazine.

AFSCME LEADER
1625 L St., NW
Washington, DC 20036-5687
(202) 429-1144
Fax: (202) 429-1084
organize!@afscme.org
http://www.afscme.org

Activist newsletter of the
American Federation of State,
County, and Municipal
Employees

AGAINST THE
CURRENT
7012 Michigan Ave.
Detroit MI 48210
(313) 841-0161
Fax: (313)841-8884
solidarity@igc.org
efc@igc.apc.org
http://www.igc.apc.org/
  solidarity

Promoting dialogue among
activists, organizers, and
serious scholars of the left,
from the general perspective
of "socialism from below."

AHORANOW
Lian Hurst Mann, Editor
3780 Wilshire Blvd., Ste 1200
Los Angeles, CA 90010
(213) 387-280
LHM1@aol.com
http://www.igc.apc.org/lctr/
  ahoranow.html

A bilingual English/Spanish
periodical about strategy and
tactics in contemporary campaigns against racism, xeno-
phobia, as well as corporate
and government attacks
against working people.

AIM: Armenian
International Magazine
P.O. Box 10793
Glendale, CA 91209-3793
(818) 246-7979;
(818) 246-0088
aim4m@well.com

A monthly magazine of news
and analysis about Armenia
and the Armenian Diaspora.

AKWESASNE NOTES
P.O. Box 196
Rooseveltown, NY 13683
(518) 358-9531; (613) 575-2935
notes@glen-net.ca

News of Mohawk and other
indigenous peoples.

ALBION MONITOR
P.O. Box 1733
Sebastopol, CA 95473
(707) 823-0100
editor@monitor.net
http://www.monitor.net/
    monitor

Primarily covering environmental News and, human
rights and politics. Syndicated
and other copyrighted material available to subscribers
only.

ALLIANCE FOR
COMMUNITY MEDIA
666 11th St., NW, Suite 806
Washington, DC 20001-45429
(202) 393-2650
Fax: (202) 393-2653
acm@alliancecm.org
http://www.alliancecm.org

Covers legal, community,
censorship, technical, professional, and advocacy issues
regarding cable access, internet and electronic media.

ALTERNATIVE PRESS
INDEX
P.O. Box 33109
Baltimore, MD 21218-0401
(410) 243-2471
Fax:(410) 235-5325
altpress@igc.apc.org
http://www.altpress.org/
Includes coverage of practices
and theories of socialism,
labor, feminism, ecology,
anarchism, anti-racism,
and more.

ALTERNATIVE PRESS
REVIEW
P.O. Box 4710
Arlington, VA 22204
(703) 553-2945
apr@flag.blackened.net
http://flag.blackened.net/apr

Publishes a wide variety of
essays from radical zines,
tabloids, books and maga-
zines, a selection of short and
lively article excerpts,
reviews, commentary and
columns on the alternative
press scene and other alternative media.

ALTERNATIVE
THERAPIES IN HEALTH
AND MEDICINE
101 Columbia
Aliso Viejo, CA 92656
(800) 899-1712
Fax: (714) 362-2020
alttherapy@aol.com
http://www.alternative/
    therapies.com

Sharing information about the
practical uses of alternative
therapies in preventing and
treating disease, healing ill-
ness, and promoting health.

ALTERNATIVES
1800 30th St., Suite 314
Boulder, CO 80301-1032
(303) 444-6684
Fax: (303) 444-0824
sbarr@rienner.com
peacock@rienner.com
http://www.rienner.com

Alternative views in international relations, politics, and Third World study.

ALTERNATIVES
1718 M St., NW, #245
Washington, DC 20036
(202) 588-9888
Fax: (202) 588-1818
NLGJA@aol.com
http://www.nlgja.org

News and reports from the National Gay and Lesbian Journalists Association.

ALTERNATIVES JOURNAL
University of Waterloo
Waterloo, ON N2L 3G1
Canada
(519) 888-4567 x6783
Fax: (519) 746-0292
alternat@fes.uwaterloo.ca
http://www.fes.uwaterloo.ca/
    alternatives

Critical and informed analysis of environmental issues.

AMERICAN EDITOR, THE
11690 B Sunrise Valley Dr.
Reston, VA 20191-1409
(703) 453-1122
Fax: (703) 453-1133
asne@asne.org
http://www.asne.org

Discusses topics related to the current state and future of U.S. newspapers and journalism.

AMERICAN
JOURNALISM REVIEW
8701 Adelphi Rd.
Adelphi, MD 20783
(301) 405-8803
Fax: (301)405-8323
editor@ajr.umd.edu
http://www.ajr.org

Reports on American journalism and provides information for professional journalists.

AMERICAN PROSPECT
P.O. Box 383080
Cambridge, MA 02238
(617) 547-2950
Fax: (617) 547-3896
prospect@epn.org
http://epn.org/prospect.html

A bi-monthly publication covering political, social and cultural issues.

AMERICAN WRITER
113 University Place, 6th fl.
New York, NY 10003
(212) 254-0279
Fax: (212) 254-0673
nwu@nwu.org
http://www.nwu.org/nwu

Tracks developments in the media/information industry and the labor movement that concern working writers.

AMICUS JOURNAL
40 West 20th St.
New York, NY 10011
(212) 727-2700 x412
Fax: (212) 727-1773

nrdrinfo@nrdc.org
http://www.nrdc.org

Focuses on thought and opinion on environmental affairs.

ANIMAL PEOPLE
P.O. Box 960
Clinton, WA 98236-0960
(360) 589-2505

An activist magazine covering animal rights and protection issues.

ANIMALS' AGENDA, THE
1301 S. Baylis St., Suite 325
P.O. Box 25881
Baltimore, MD 21224
(410) 675-4566
Fax: (410) 675-0066
office@animalsagenda.org

Bimonthly news magazine dedicated to informing people about animal rights and cruelty-free living for the purpose of inspiring activism for animals.

ANNALS OF IMPROBABLE RESEARCH
P.O. Box 380853
Cambridge, MA 02238
(617) 491-4437
Fax: (617) 661-0927
air@improb.com
http://www.improb.com

A humor magazine about science, technology and medicine.

ANTIPODE
238 Main St.
Malden, MA 02148
imcla@blackwell.com
http://www.blackwellpub.com
(800) 835-6770
Fax: (781) 388-8210

Marxist, socialist, anarchist, anti-racist, and feminist analysis of environmental and geographical issues.

ARAB AMERICAN NEWS
5461 Schaefer Road
Dearborn, MI 48121
(313) 582-4888
Fax: (313) 582-7870
kaysaan@aol.com
http://www.arabamerican
    news.com

Nationally circulated, bilingual weekly newspaper serving the nation's three million Arab Americans.

ARMS SALES MONITOR
307 Massachusetts Ave., NE
Washington, DC 20002
(202) 675-1018
Fax: (202) 675-1010
llumpe@fas.org
http://www.fas.org/asmp/

Highlights U.S. government policies on arms exports and conventional weapons proliferation.

ASIANWEEK
809 Sacramento St.
San Francisco, CA 94108
(415) 397-0220
Fax: (415) 397-7258

A nationally circulated
publication with a
"community" focus,
covering news of Asian
Americans.

BAFFLER, THE
P.O. Box 378293
Chicago, IL 60637
(773) 493-0413
Fax: (773) 493-0515
info@thebaffler.org
http://www.thebaffler.org

An independent journal
of cultural criticism and
literature.

BEAT WITHIN, THE
450 Mission St., #204
San Francisco, CA 94105
(415) 243-4364
yo@pacificnews.org
http://www.pacificnews.org/y
o/beat/

A weekly newsletter
of writing and art by
incarcerated youth.

BEYOND TV
2311 Kimball Place
Silver Springs, MD 20910
(301) 588-4001
(301) 588-4001
apluhar@tvp.org
http://www.tvp.org

Quarterly newsletter aimed
at empowering parents to use
television wisely.

BIRACIAL CHILD
P.O. Box 17479
Beverly Hills, CA 90209
(213) 251-3805

A quarterly geared toward
parents of biracial children
and the broad subjects and
issues that these children
face.

BITCH: Feminist Response
to Pop Culture
3128 16th St., Box 143
San Francisco, CA 94103
ljervis@sirius.com

Devoted to feminist analysis
of movies, television,
advertising, magazines, and
sociocultural trends. Also
spotlights women making
alternative, progressive
media.

BLACK CHILD
P.O. Box 17479
Beverly Hills, CA 90209
(213) 251-3805

A bi-monthly geared toward
African American parents and
the broad subjects and issues
that black parents face.

BLACK ENTERPRISE
130 Fifth Ave.
New York, NY 10011
(212) 242-8000

Fax: (212) 886-9610
sobers@blackenterprise.com
http://www.blackenterprise.
  com

Targeted to black
professionals.

BLACK ISSUES IN HIGHER
EDUCATION
10520 Warwick Ave.
Suite B-8
Fairfax, VA 22030-3136
(703) 385-2981
Fax: (703) 385-1839
bi@cmadiccw.com
www.blackissues.com

Bi-weekly—the nation's only
news magazine dedicated
exclusively to minority issues
in higher education.

BLACK MASKS
P.O. Box 2
Bronx, NY 10471
(212) 304-8900
Fax: (212) 304-8900

One of the most extensive
bi-monthly publications
devoted to the Black
performing and visual arts
in the United States.

BLACK RENAISSANCE/
RENAISSANCE NOIRE
601 North Morton
Bloomington, IN 47404
(800) 842-6796
Fax: (812) 855-8507

Essays, fiction, reviews, and
art work that address the full
range of contemporary Black
concerns.

BLACK SCHOLAR
P.O. Box 2869
Oakland, CA 94618-0069
(510) 547-6633
Fax: (510) 547-6679
blkschlr@aol.com
http://www.z.blackscholar.org

An independent intellectual
journal of the African-
American experience.

BLK
P.O. Box 83912
Los Angeles, CA 90083-0912
(310) 410-0808
Fax: (310) 410-9250
newsroom@blk.com
http://www.blk.com

News magazine for black,
lesbian and gay community.

BODY POLITIC, THE
P.O. Box 2363
Bighamton, NY 13902
(607) 648-2760
Fax: (607) 648-2511
annebower@mindspring.com
http://www.bodypolitic.org/

A national abortion and health
care rights news service.

BORDER/LINES
400 Dover Court Rd.
Toronto, ON M67 3E7
Canada
(416) 534-3224
Fax: (416) 534-2301
borderln@idirect.com
http://www.interlog.com/
    ~kavik/border.htm

Designed to fill the space
between academic journals
and specialist cultural
magazines.

BOSTON REVIEW
E53-407, MIT
Cambridge, MA 02139
(617) 253-3642
Fax: (617) 252-1549
BBR-info@BostonBookReview.
    com
http://www.bookwire.com/
    bbr-home.html

Combines commitments to
public reason with literary
imagination.

BOYCOTT QUARTERLY
P.O. Box 30727
Seattle, WA 98103-0727
boycottguy@aol.com

Comprehensive coverage of
boycotts across the political
spectrum and around the
world.

BRAZZIL
2039 North Ave.
Los Angeles, CA 90042-1024
(213) 255-8062
Fax: (213) 257-3487
brazzil@brazzil.com
http://www.brazzil.com

In-depth articles deal with
politics, economy, behavior,
ecology, tourism, literature,
arts and culture.

BREAKTHROUGH
P.O. Box 1442
San Francisco, CA 94114

A magazine of international
and domestic politics and
activism.

BRIARPATCH
2138 McIntyre St.
Regine, SK S4P 2R7 Canada
(316) 525-2949
Fax: (306) 565-3430

Alternative view on issues,
events and Aboriginal and
women's rights.

BRILL'S CONTENT
521 5th Ave., 11th Floor
New York, NY 10175
(800) 829-9154; (212) 824-1900
Fax: (904) 445-2728
http://www.brillscontent.com

A monthly magazine based
on the idea that consumers of
news and information should
know how media is produced
and how reliable it is.

BROADCASTING AND
CABLE MAGAZINE
1705 DeSales St., NW, Ste 600
Washington, DC 20036
(202) 659-2340
Fax: (202) 429-0651
editor@broadcastingcable.com
http://www.broadcasting
    cable.com

A newsweekly on
broadcasting and cable issues.

BROKEN PENCIL
P.O. Box 203, Stn.P
Toronto, ON M5S 2S7
Canada
(416) 340-0878
Fax: (416) 340-0878
editor@brokenpencil.com
http://www.brokenpencil.com

Reprints of the best of the
underground press and original features.

BULLETIN, THE
1904 Franklin St., #505
Oakland, CA 94612
pbiusa@igc.apc.org
http://www.igc.org/pbi.html.

Provides in-depth information
on a monthly basis to subscribers with more extensive
knowledge about the regions
in which PBI works.

BULLETIN IN DEFENSE
OF MARXISM
P.O. Box 1317
New York, NY 10009

Issues of the global and
domestic class struggle from
the perspective of the
American Trotskyist
tradition.

BULLETIN OF
CONCERNED ASIAN
SCHOLARS
1515 Webster St., # 305
Oakland, CA 94612
(510) 451-1742
Fax: (510) 835-9631
tfenton@igc.org

Challenging accepted form-
ulas for understanding Asia,
the world, and ourselves.

BULLETIN OF THE
ATOMIC SCIENTISTS
6042 South Kimbark Ave.
Chicago, IL 60637
(773) 702-2555
Fax: (773) 702-0725
bullatomsci@igc.apc.org
http://www.bullatomsci.org

Covers international security,
military affairs, nuclear
issues.

BUSINESS ETHICS
2845 Harriet Ave, #207
P.O. Box 8439
Minneapolis, MN 55408
(612) 879-0695
Fax: (612) 879-0699
BizEthics@aol.com

The mission of BE is to
promote ethical business
practices.

CALIFORNIA PRISON
FOCUS
2940 16th St., Rm. 100
San Fransisco, CA 94110
(415) 252-9211
coreman@igc.org

A newsletter that spreads
information about control
unit prisons, conditions in
California, and provides a
voice for the prisoners.

CALYPSO LOG
870 Greenbrier Cir., Ste 402
Chesapeake, VA 23320
(757) 523-9335
Fax: (757) 523-2747
cousteau@infi.net
http://www.cousteau.org

Focused on protection and
improvement of the quality of
life for future generations.

CANADIAN DIMENSION
2B-91 Albert St.
Winnipeg, MB R3B IG5
Canada
(204) 957-1519
Fax: (204) 943-4617
info@canadiandimension.
mb.ca
http://www.canadiandimen
sion.mb.ca/index/html

Principled and independent
hard news and analysis from
a left-wing perspective—
multiple winner of Project
Censored's Canada awards.

CAPITAL EYE
1320 19 St., NW, #620
Washington, DC 20036
(202) 857-0044
Fax: (202) 857-7809
info@crp.org
http://www.crp.org

Covers money-in-politics at
the federal, state, and local
levels.

CAQ
1500 Massachusetts Ave.,
NW, #732
Washington, DC 20005
(202) 331-9763
Fax: (202) 331-9751
caq@igc.apc.org
http://www.caq.com

Investigative journalism
exposing malfeasance and
covert activities in government, corporations, and other
areas affecting the public.

CENSORSHIP NEWS
275 7th Ave., 20th Floor
New York, NY 10001
(212) 807-6222
Fax: (212) 807-6245
ncac@ncac.org
http://www.ncac.com

Contains information and
discussion about freedom of
expression issues.

CHALLENGE
150 W. 28th St., Room 301
New York, NY 10001-6103
(212) 255-3959

A revolutionary communist
newspaper.

CHILD OF COLORS
P.O. Box 17479
Beverly Hills, CA 90209
(213) 251-3805

Quarterly magazine dealing
with issues facing and of
concern to parents and
children of color.

CHRISTIAN SCIENCE
MONITOR
1 Norway St.
Boston, MA 02115-3195
(800) 288-7090; (617) 450-2000
orders@csmonitor.com
http://www.csmonitor.com

An 87-year-old daily newspaper covering national and
international news.

CHRONICLE OF HIGHER
EDUCATION, THE
1255 23rd St., NW
Washington, DC 20037
(202) 466-1000
Fax: (202) 296-2691
editor@chronicle.com
http://www.chronicle.com

The number one news source
for college and university
faculty.

CHRONICLE OF
PHILANTHROPY, THE
1255 23rd St., NW, 7th Floor
Washington, DC 20037
(202) 466-1200
Fax: (202) 466-2078
editor@philanthropy.com
http://www.philanthropy.com

Published bi-monthly, this
newspaper of the non-profit
world is the number one
news source for charity leaders and fund raisers.

CINEASTE
200 Park Ave. South
Suite 1601
New York, NY 10003
(212) 982-1241
Fax: (212) 982-1241
cineaste@cineasuitecom

Art and politics of the
cinema.

CIVIL LIBERTIES
125 Broad St.
New York, NY 10004
(212) 549-2500
Fax: (212) 549-2646
http://www.aclu.org

Issues of civil liberties including online information on
Internet free speech issues.

COLORLINES MAGAZINE
4096 Piedmont Ave.
Suite 319
Oakland, CA 94611
(510) 653-3415
Fax: (510) 653-3427

colorlines@arc.org
http://www.arc.org

The nation's premier magazine on race, culture and organizing. Showcases the new race intellectuals, critiques compelling music, arts, books and film, and documents the movement for social change.

COLUMBIA JOURNALISM REVIEW
700 Journalism Building
New York, NY 10027
(212) 854-1881
Fax: (212) 854-8580
http://www.cjr.org

Assesses the performance of journalism and stimulates continuing improvements in the profession.

COMMUNITIES MAGAZINE
P.O. Box 169
Masonville, CO 80541
(970) 593-5615
Fax: (970) 593-5615
communities@igc.org
http://www.ic.org

Focus on "intentional communities," including ecovillages, co-housing, urban housing cooperatives, shared living and other projects.

COMMUNITY MEDIA REVIEW
666 11st. NW, Suite 806
Washington, DC 20001
(202) 393-2650
Fax: (202) 393-2653
AllianceCM@aol.com
http://www.thesphere.com/
    ACTV/acm.html

A newsletter reporting on political and regulatory issues in the media; reports on emerging information systems.

COMPARATIVE STUDIES:
South Africa, Asia, & the Middle East
P.O. Box 90660
Durham, NC 90660
(919) 687-3614
http://Ki.acupub.duke.edu
http://www.duke.edu/web/
    dupress

Comparative studies of South Asia, Africa, and the Middle East.

CONGRESSIONAL QUARTERLY WEEKLY REPORT
1414 22nd St., NW
Washington, DC 20037
(202) 887-8500
Fax: (202) 728-1863
http://voter96.cqalert.com

A world-class provider of information on government, politics, and public policy.

CONSCIOUS CHOICE
920 North Franklin St.
Suite 202
Chicago, IL 60610-3119
(312) 440-4373
Fax: (312) 751-3973
cc@consciouschoice.com or
james@consciouschoice.com
http://www.cosciouschoice.
   com

Promotes sustainable patterns
of living, environmental issues
and natural alternatives,
natural health, living and
vegetarian nutrition.

CONSUMER REPORTS
101 Truman Ave.
Yonkers, NY 10703-1057
(914) 378-2000
Fax: (914) 378-2992
http://www.consumerreports.
   org

A nonprofit organization that
has been testing products on
behalf of consumers for more
than 60 years.

CO-OP AMERICA
QUARTERLY
1612 K St. NW, Suite 600
Washington, DC 20006
(800) 58-GREEN
(202) 872-5307
Fax: (202) 331-8166
info@coopamerica.org
http://www.coopamerica.org

Teaches consumers how
to use their spending power
to support socially and
environmentally responsible
businesses and promote
social and economic justice.

CORPORATE CRIME
REPORTER
1209 National Press Building
Washington, DC 20045
(202) 737-1680

Legal weekly covering issues
of corporate and white-collar
crime.

COUNTERPOISE
1716 Williston Road
Gainesville, FL 32608
(352) 335-2200
willett@gnv.fdt.net
http://www.jessamyn.com/
   srrt/aip/counterpoise.html

Sponsored by the Alternatives
in Print Task Force of the
Social Responsibilities Round
Table of the American Library
Association.

COUNTERPUNCH
3220 N St., NW, Suite 346
Washington, DC 20007
(800) 840-3683
Fax: (503) 657-0096
counterpunch@counterpunch.
   org
http://www.counterpunch.org

DC-based investigative
newsletter on power and evil
in Washington.

CRONE CHRONICLES:
A Journal of Conscious Aging
Box 81
Jackson, WY 83011
(307) 733-5409
Fax: (307) 733-8639
http://www.feminist.com/
  crone.html

A grassroots publication
written by and for honest,
outrageous, and wise older
women who are challenging
stereotypes by living
authentically.

CUBA UPDATE
124 West 23rd St.
New York, NY 10011
(212) 242-0559
Fax: 212) 2(42-1937
cubanctr@igc.apc.org
http://www.eden.com/fine
  print/40289.html

Provides accurate, accessible
news coverage and discussion
of important issues almost
impossible to find elsewhere.

CULTURAL
ENVIRONMENT
MONITOR, THE
3508 Market St., Suite 30-030
Philadelphia, PA 19104
(215) 204-6434
Fax: (215) 387-1560
cem@libertynet.org
http://www.cemnet.org

Newsletter of the Cultural
Environment Movement.

CULTURAL SURVIVAL
QUARTERLY
96 Mt. Auburn St.
Cambridge, MA 02138
(617) 441-5400
Fax: (617) 441-5417
csinc@cs.org
http://www.cs.org/csq/
  csq.html

World report on the rights of
indigenous peoples and ethnic
minorities.

CULTURE WATCH
1904 Franklin St., Suite 900
Oakland, CA 94612
(510) 835-4692
Fax: (510) 835-3017
masildatactr@tmn.com
http://www.egc.org/culture
  watch/

Monthly newsletter which
tracks and monitors the
political and social agenda
of the religious right.

DARK NIGHT PRESS
P.O. Box 3629
Chicago, IL 60690-3629
(207) 839-5794
darknight@igc.org

Supports the struggles for
liberation of indigenous
peoples, and thereby human
liberation, by addressing
the factors and conditions
that make these struggles
necessary. Publishes *Dark
Night Field Notes*.

DAYBREAK
P.O. Box 315
Williamsville, NY 14231
(716) 645-2548
Fax: (716) 645-5977

Forum of information
sharing around issues which
impact indigenous peoples
worldwide.

DEFENSE MONITOR
1779 Massachusetts Ave.
Suite 615
Washington, DC 20036
(202) 332-0600
Fax: (202) 462-4559
info@cdi.org
http://www.cdi.org

Opposes policies that increase
the danger of war.

DEMOCRATIC LEFT
180 Varick St.
12th Floor
New York, NY 10014
(212) 727-8610
Fax: (212) 727-8616
dsa@dsausa.org
http://www.dsausa.org/
    index.html

A quarterly review of socialist
issues and activities.

DETODO UN POCO
2830 5th St.
Boulder, CO 80304
(303) 444-8565
Fax: (303) 545-2074
tmoore@igc.apc.org

Issues in Central America,
Mexico, the Caribbean, and
U.S. influence in the region.

DIOXIN DIGEST
150 S. Washington St., #300
Falls Church, VA 22040
(703) 237-2249
Fax: (703) 237-8389
cchw@essential.org
http://www.essential.org/
    cchw&sustain.org/hcwh

A free publication providing
information on Dioxin and
other chemical toxins.

DISSENT
521 Fifth Ave., Suite 1700
New York, NY 10017
(212) 595-3084
Fax: (212) 595-3084
dissent@igc.org
http://www.igc.org/dissent

Quarterly democratic
socialist and left-liberal
argument.

DIVERSITY SUPPLIERS
& BUSINESS MAGAZINE
P.O. Box 579
Winchester, CA 92596
(909) 926-2119

Addresses issues vital to all
suppliers and purchasers of
products and services of
established and/or new and
growing diverse businesses.

DOLLARS AND SENSE:
WHAT'S LEFT IN
ECONOMICS
1 Summer St.
Somerville, MA 02143
(617) 628-8411
Fax: (617) 628-2025
dollars@igc.apc.org
http://www.igc.org/dollars

Reports on issues of social
justice and economic policy.

DOMES
P.O. Box 413
Milwaukee, WI 53201
(414) 229-4709
Fax: (414) 229-4848

Quarterly provides for a
balance of views on the
Middle East.

DOUBLE TAKE
1317 West Pettigrew St.
Durham, NC 27705
(919) 660-3669
Fax: (919) 660-3688
dtmag@aol.com
http://www.duke.edu/
    doubletake/
Publishes work in the
documentary tradition
including fiction, non-fiction,
reportage, poetry, and
photography.

E: THE ENVIRONMENTAL
MAGAZINE
P.O. Box 5098
Westport, CT 06881
(203) 854-5559
Fax: (203) 866-0602

Emagazine@prodigy.net
http://emagazine.com

Independent national
environmental magazine.

EARTH FIRST! JOURNAL
P.O. Box 1415
Eugene, OR 97440
(541) 344-8004
Fax: (541) 344-7688
earthfirst@igc.apc.org
http://www.enviroweb.org/ef/

Reports on the radical environmental movement and
hard-to-find information
about strategies to stop the
destruction of the planet.

EARTH ISLAND JOURNAL
300 Broadway, Suite 28
San Francisco, CA 94133
(415) 788-3666
Fax: (415) 788-7324
journal@earthisland.org
http://www.earthisland.org/

A quarterly publication of the
Earth Island Institute that
covers the broad range of
environmental issues from
urban toxics to wilderness
preservation to the
militarization of space.

ECOLOGIST, THE
Cisbury House, Furze View
5 Oaks Rd.
Slinford, West Sussex
RH13 7RH
UK
(617) 253-2889

Fax: (617) 258-6779
ecologist@gn.apc.org
http://gold.net/ecosystem/
    ecol.htm

Covers ecological issues
and supports small-scale
agriculture and democratized
political power.

EEO BIMONTHLY
1800 Sherman Pl.
Suite 300
Evanston, IL 60201-3769
(847) 475-8800
Fax: (847) 475-8807
National Equal Employment

Opportunity Career Journal,
addresses the career development needs of today's diverse
professional multi-ethnic
work force.

EIDOS MAGAZINE
P.O. Box 96,
Boston, MA 02137-0096
(617) 262-0096
Fax: (617) 364-0096
eidos@eidos.org
http://www.eidos.org

Advocates and defends
sexual freedom as a human,
constitutional and civil right.

EL INFORMADOR
HISPANO
2229 N. Main St.
Fort Worth, TX 76106
(817) 626-8624
Fax: (817) 626-8635

Promotes professional
development of the Latino
media in the United States.

EL MUNDO
630 20th St.
Oakland, CA 94612
(510) 287-8200
Fax: (510) 763-9670

A national Spanish language
weekly publication.

EL SALVADOR WATCH
19 West 21st St., Room 502
New York, NY 10010
(212) 229-1290
Fax: (212) 645-7280
cispesnatl@igc.org
http://www.cispes.org

A grassroots organization
dedicated to supporting the
Salvadoran people's struggle
for self-determination and
social and economic justice.

EL PREGONERO
5001 Eastern Ave.
Hyattsville, MD 20782
(301) 853-4504
Fax: (301) 853-3349
Hispanic tabloid newspaper.

EMERGE: Black America's
News Magazine
One B.E.T. Plaza
1900 West Place, NE
Washington, DC 20018
(202) 608-2093
Fax: (202) 608-2598
emergmag@aol.com

News analysis and commentary from the African-American perspective.

**ENVIRONMENTAL
HEALTH MONTHLY**
150 S. Washington St., #300
Falls Church, VA 22040
(703) 237-2249
Fax: (703) 237-8389
cchw@essential.org
http://essential.org/cchw

A monthly digest of reprinted environmental, medical, and scientific articles on a particular topic.

ESSENCE MAGAZINE
1500 Broadway
New York, NY 10036
(212) 642-0600
http://essence.com

News and commentary for African American women.

EVERYBODY'S:
The Caribbean-American
Magazine
1630 Nostrand Ave.
Brooklyn, NY 11226
(718) 941-1879
Fax: (718) 941-1886
A general interest Caribbean/American monthly magazine.

EVERYONE'S BACKYARD
P.O. Box 6806
Falls Church, VA 22040
(703) 237-2249
Fax: (703) 237-8389

cchw@essential.org
http://essential.org/cchw

The Journal of the Grassroots Movement for Environmental Justice.

EXTRA!
130 West 25th St.
New York, NY 10001
(212) 633-6700
Fax: (212) 727-7668
info@fair.org
http://www.fair.org

Provides media criticism featuring impeccably researched articles on biased reporting, censored news, media mergers, and more.

EYE MAGAZINE
301 South Elm St., Suite 405
Greensboro, NC 27401
(336) 370-1702
Fax: (336) 370-1603
eye@nr.infi.net

Covers film, technology, science, conspiracies, retro TV, animal rights, medicine and culture.

FACTNET NEWSLETTER
P.O. Box 3135
Boulder, CO 80307-3135
factnet@factnet.org
http://www.factsheet5.com

Protecting freedom of mind by exposing cults and mind control.

FACTSHEET 5
P.O. Box 170099
San Francisco, CA
94117-0099
(415) 668-1781
seth@factsheet5.com
http://factsheet.5.com

Guide to the 'zine revolution
featuring resources and
reviews of thousands of
underground publications.

FAT!SO?
P.O. Box 423464
San Francisco, CA 94142
(800) OHFATSO
marilyn@fatso.com
http://www.fatso.com

For people who don't
apologize for their size.

FELLOWSHIP MAGAZINE
521 North Broadway
Nyack, NY 10960
(914) 358-4601
Fax: (914) 358-4924
fellowship@igc.org
http://www.nonviolence.org/
    for/fellowship

Seeks to replace violence,
war, racism, and economic
injustice with nonviolence,
peace, and justice.

FEMINIST MAJORITY
REPORT
1600 Wilson Boulevard, #801
Arlington, VA 22209
(703) 522-2214
http://www.feminist.org

News and reports on politics,
culture, women's health,
reproductive rights, events,
career opportunities, and the
multi-dimensional nature of
feminism.

FIFTH ESTATE
4632 Second Ave.
Detroit, MI 48201
(313) 831-6800

Longest-running English
language anarchist
publication in the U.S.

FILIPINAS MAGAZINE
655 Sutter St., Suite 333
San Francisco, CA 94102
(415) 563-5878
Fax: (415) 292-5993

Covers Filipino American
interests and affairs.

FILIPINO EXPRESS, THE
2711 Kennedy Blvd.
Jersey City, NJ 07306
(201) 333-5709
Fax: (201) 434-0880
Weekly publication for
Asian/Pacific Islanders.

FILIPINO REPORTER
350 5th Ave., Suite 610
Empire State Bldg.
New York, NY 10018
(212) 967-5784
Fax: (212) 967-5848

English-language weekly
of particular interest to
Asian/Pacific Islanders.

FIRE INSIDE, THE
100 McAllister St.
San Francisco, CA 94102
(415) 255-7036 x4
Fax: (415) 552-3150
ccwp@igc.org
http://www.prison=
    activist.org/ccwp

A quarterly newsletter
covering issues related to
incarcerated women.

FIRE WEED
P.O. Box 279, Station B
Toronto, ON M5Y 2W2
Canada
(416) 504 1339

A feminist quarterly of
writing, politics, art and
culture.

FIRST THINGS: A Journal
Of Religion And Public Life
156 5th Ave., Suite 400
New York, NY 10010

Dedicated to advancing a
religiously-informed public
philosophy.

FOOD FIRST NEWS
398 60th St.
Oakland, CA 94618
(510) 654-4400
Fax: (510) 654-4551
foodfirst@sirius.com
http://www.foodfirst.org

An information and action
guide for ending world hunger
and poverty.

FOOD NOT BOMBS MENU
3145 Geary Boulevard, #12
San Francisco, CA 94118
(800) 884-1136
foodnotbombs@earthlink.net
http://www.eci.com/dave/
    fnb.html

Reprints flyers, letters, and
news reports about Food Not
Bombs, Homes Not Jails, the
free radio movement, and
other information about the
direct action community.

FOOD & WATER JOURNAL
389 VT Rte. 215
Walden, VT 05873
(802) 563-3300
Fax: (802) 563-3310

A quarterly magazine which
advocates for safe food and
water.

FORT APACHE SCOUT
P.O. Box 898
Whiteriver, AZ 85941-0898
(602) 338-4813
Fax: (602) 338-4778

The official newspaper of the
White Mountain Apache
Tribe also contains a section
devoted to national Indian
news stories.

FORWARD
45 East 33rd St.
New York, NY 10016
(212) 889-8200
Fax: (212) 447-6406

Weekly dedicated to social justice and helping generations of immigrant Jews enter American life.

FREEDOM SOCIALIST NEWSPAPER
1018 Rainier Ave. South
Seattle, WA 98118
(206) 722-2453
freedomsoc@igc.org
http://www.socialism.com

An international socialist feminist quarterly providing news, analysis, reviews and humor aimed at ridding the world of bigots, bosses, and patriarchs. Special attention to the issues and leadership of women, people of color, and sexual minorities.

FREE INQUIRY: The International Secular Humanist Magazine
P.O. Box 664
Amherst, NY 14226
(716) 636-7571
Fax: (716) 636-1733
http://www.secularhuman
    ism.org

A quarterly magazine which celebrates reason and humanity.

FRONTIERS NEWS MAGAZINE
P.O. Box 46367
West Hollywood, CA 90046
(213) 848-2222
Fax: (213) 656-8784

webmaster@frontiersweb.com
http://www.frontiersweb.com

A comprehensive magazine for and about lesbian/gay issues and rights.

FUSE MAGAZINE
401 Richmond St. W.
Suite 454
Toronto, ON M5V 3A8
Canada
(416) 340-8026
Fax: (416) 340-0494
fuse@interlog.com

Blending critical analysis of contemporary art, *Fuse* focuses on cultural politics and the relationship between art and social change.

GENEWATCH
5 Upland Road
Suite 3
Cambridge, MA 02140
(617) 868-0870
Fax: (617) 491-5344
crg@essential.org
http://www.essential.org/crg

Provides information and opinions about the social and environmental aspects of genetic engineering.

GEO—GRASSROOTS ECONOMIC ORGANIZING
83 Charles Lane
Storrs, CT 06268
(860) 429-6194
krimerm@uconnvm.edu

A bi-monthly newsletter dedicated to educating the public about how to organize effectively.

GLAADLINES
150 West 26th St., Suite 503
New York, NY 10001
(212) 807-1700
Fax: (212) 807-1806
glaad@glaad.org
http://www.glaad.org

An on-line resource for promoting fair, accurate, and inclusive media representation of lesbian, gay, bisexual, and transgendered people.

GLOBAL PESTICIDE CAMPAIGNER
49 Powell St., Suite 500
San Francisco, CA 94105
(415) 981-1771
Fax: (415) 981-1991
panna@panna.org
http://www.panna.org/panna

Environmental, health, and other information about pesticides, ecological pest control, and sustainable agriculture.

GNOSIS MAGAZINE
P.O. Box 1427
San Francisco, CA 94114
(415) 974-0600
Fax: (415) 974-0366
gnosis@well.com
http://www.lumen.org

Devoted to the exploration of spiritual and esoteric paths of Western Civilization.

GOVERNMENT INFORMATION INSIDER
1742 Connecticut Ave., NW
Washington, DC 20009
(202) 234-8494
Fax: (202) 234-8584
ombwatch@ombwatch.org
http://www.ombwatch.org/

A magazine which focuses on government secrecy and the public's right to know.

GRASSROOTS FUNDRAISING JOURNAL
P.O. Box 11607
Berkeley, CA 94712
(510) 704-8714
Fax: (510) 649-7913
chardn@aol.com
http://www.chardonpress.com

Grassroots Fundraising Journal is a how-to magazine providing information on all aspects of fundraising for groups working for social change.

GREENPAGES
P.O. Box 5631
Santa Monica, CA 90409
(310) 392-8450
greenpages@greens.org
http://www.greenparties.org

Newsletter of the Association of State Green Parties,

featuring news of the Green Party in the United States and abroad.

GROUNDWORK
Tides Center
P.O. Box 14141
San Francisco, CA 94114
(415) 255-7623

Covers community organizing and direct action on environmental and social justice issues.

GUILD NOTES
126 University Place
5th Floor
New York, NY 10003
(212) 627-2656
Fax: (212) 627-2404
nlgno@nlg.org
http://www.nlg.org

Newsletter of the National Lawyer's Guild.

HA!
P.O. Box 1282
Carrboro, NC 97510
gmonster@email.unc.edu
http://www.unc.edu/~cheryll

A 'zine for women's self-expression.

HARD HAT MAGAZINE
P.O. Box 40668
San Francisco, CA 94140
(415) 621-8468
Fax: (415) 648-9062
hardhat@insinex.com

A construction workers union support magazine.

HEALTH QUEST:
The Publication
of Black Wellness
200 Highpoint Dr.
Suite 215
Chalfont, PA 18914
(215) 822-7935
Fax: (215) 997-9582

Focuses specifically on health and wellness in the African-American community.

HEART & SOUL
33 East Minor St.
Emmaus, PA 18098
(610) 967-5171

National/Bi-Monthly. Addresses well-being of body, mind, and spirit for African American women.

HIGH COUNTRY NEWS
P.O. Box 1090
Paonia, CO 81428
(970) 527-4898
editor@hcn.org
http://www.hcn.org

Bi-weekly newspaper that reports environmental news, analysis and commentary on water, logging, wildlife, grazing, wilderness, growth and other issues changing the face of the West.

HIGH GRADER
MAGAZINE
P.O. Box 714
Colbalt, ON P0J 1C0
Canada
(705) 679-5533
Fax: (705) 679-5033
News reporting and offbeat
cultural comments from a
working-class perspective.

HIGHTOWER
LOWDOWN, THE
P.O. Box 20065
New York, NY 10011
(212) 228-9070
Fax: (212) 979-2055
lowdown@newslet.com

A twice-monthly populist
newsletter featuring Jim
Hightower.

HIP MAMA
P.O. Box 9097
Oakland, CA 94613
(800) 585-6262
hipmama@sirius.com
http://www.hipmama.com

A 'zine for progressive families covering the culture and
politics of parenting.

HISPANIC ENGINEER
729 East Pratt St.
Suite 504
Baltimore, MD 21202
(410) 244-7101
Fax: (410) 752-1837
ccgmag@aol.com
http://www.ccgmag.com

This quarterly is dedicated
to promotion opportunities
for Hispanic Americans in
science and technology.

HUMAN EVENTS
MAGAZINE
1 Massachusetts NW
Washington, DC 20001
(202) 216-0600
Fax: (202) 216-0611

A national conservative
weekly with political analysis
and inquiry.

HUMAN QUEST
1074 23rd Ave. North
Petersburg, FL 33704-3228
(813) 894-0097
An independent journal
of religious humanism.

HUMAN RIGHTS TRIBUNE
8 York St., Suite 302
Ottawa, ON K1N 5S6
Canada
(613) 789-7407
Fax: (613) 789-7414
hri@hri.ca
http://www.hri.ca

Web site has links to human
rights, web sites worldwide,
job postings from human
rights organizations, databas-
es, etc.

HUMANIST IN CANADA
P.O. Box 3769, Station C
Ottawa, ON, K1Y 4J8 Canada
(613) 749-8929
Fax: (613) 749-8929

heesnaps@magi.com

With a balance of reason and compassion, this quarterly promotes critical thinking.

HUNGRY MIND REVIEW
1648 Grand Ave.
Paul, MN 55105
(612) 699-2610
Fax: (612) 699-0970
hmreview@winternet.com
http://www.bookwire.com/
    hmr

A quarterly book review magazine geared toward the iconoclastic reader who frequents independent bookstores.

I.F. MAGAZINE
2200 Wilson Boulevard
Suite 102-231
Arlington, VA 22201
(800) 738-1812
Fax: (703) 920-0946
rparry@ix.retcom.com
http://www.delve.com/
    consort.html

A bi-monthly publication of investigative journalism.

IMAGES
150 West 26th St.
Suite 503
New York, NY 10001
(212) 807-1700
Fax: (212) 807-1806
glad@glad.org
http://www.glad.org

A quarterly publication focussing on images and representations of gays, lesbians, bisexuals, and transgender people in the media.

IN THESE TIMES
2040 North Milwaukee Ave.
2nd Floor
Chicago, IL 60647-4002
(773) 772-0100
Fax: (773) 772-4180
itt@inthesetimes.com
http://www.inthesetimes.com

Independent news and views published biweekly by the Institute for Public Affairs.

INDEPENDENT FILM
& VIDEO MONTHLY
625 Broadway
9th Floor
New York, NY 10012
(212) 807-1400
Fax: (212) 463-8519
http://www.aivf.org

A monthly publication covering issues and events related to independent films and videos.

INDEPENDENT
POLITIC NEWS
P.O. Box 170610
Brooklyn, NY 11217-0610
(718) 624-1807
Fax: (718) 643-8265
indpol@igc.apc.org

Reports on building a unified, independent, progressive alternative to the corporate-controlled Democrat/Republican system.

INDIA ABROAD
43 West 24th St.
New York, NY 10010
(212) 929-1727
Fax: (212) 627-9503

General interest homeland news for Indians living in America, Canada, and England.

INDIA CURRENTS
P.O. Box 21285
San Jose, CA 95151
(408) 274-6966
Fax: (408) 274-2733

Devoted to the exploration of the arts and culture of India as it exists in the United States.

INDIA WORLDWIDE
244 Fifth Ave.
New York, NY 10001
(212) 481-3433
Fax: (212) 889-5774

A monthly publication for people of Indian descent.

INDIAN COUNTRY TODAY
(Lakota Times)
1920 Lombardy Dr.
P.O. Box 2180
Rapid City, SD 57709
(605) 341-0011

Fax: (605) 341-6940

Most influential and widely read Native American newspaper in the United States. (Also has a regional section covering the Pine Ridge Reservation.)

INDUSTRIAL WORKER
103 West Michigan Ave.
Ypsilanti, MI 48197-5438
(734) 483-3548
Fax: (734) 483-4050
ghq@iww.org
http://www.iww.org/

The monthly newspaper of the industrial workers of the world, or Wobblies.

INFOACTIVE KIDS
1511 K St., NW, Suite 518
Washington, DC 20005
(202) 628-2620
Fax: (202) 628-2554
cme@cme.org
http://www.cme.org/cme

For the child advocacy, consumer, health, and educational communities as well as a resource for journalists covering children and media topics.

INFUSION: Tools For Action And Education Newsletter
P.O. Box 425748
Cambridge, MA 02142
(617) 725-2886
cco@igc.apc.org
http://www.cco.org

Provides news, analysis, action guides, and organizing tips and resources for progressive campus activists.

INROADS
3777 Kent St., Suite A
Montreal, PQ H3S 1N4
Canada
(514 731-2691
Fax: (514) 731-8256

A literary annual in which knowledgeable Canadians with different viewpoints address political, social and economic issues.

INSIDE TRANSPORTATION
1000 Vermont Ave. NW
Suite 900
Washington, DC 20005
(202) 628-9262
ttd@ttd.org
http://www.ttd.org

Official publication of the Transportation Trades Department, AFL-CIO.

INSIGHT
3600 New York Ave., NE
Washington, DC 20002
(202) 636-8810
Fax: (202) 529-2484
76353.2113@compuserve.com
http://www.insightmag.com

Reports news that "others won't or can't." Follows stories "wherever the facts lead and regardless of who's involved."

INTELLECTUAL FREEDOM
ACTION NEWS
50 E. Huron St.
Chicago, IL 60611
(800) 545-2433 x4221
crobinson@ala.org
http://www.ala.org/alaorg/
    oif/ifan_pub.html

A monthly publication dedicated to freedom of thought, freedom of the written and spoken word, and freedom of expression.

INTELLIGENCE REPORT
400 Washington Ave.
Montgomery, AL 36104
(334) 264-0286
Fax: (334) 264-8891
http://www.splcenter.org/

Reports on white supremacist organizations and extreme anti-government groups.

INTERNATIONAL
EXAMINER
622 S. Washington St.
Seattle, WA 98104
(206) 624-3925
Fax: (206) 624-3046
Published since 1974, the *International Examiner* is the oldest English language Asian community newspaper.

INTERNATIONAL JOURNAL
OF HEALTH SERVICES
P.O. Box 337
Amityville, NY 11701
(516) 691-1270
Fax: (516) 691-1770

baywood@baywood.com
http://www.baywood.com

A journal of health and social policy, political economy, sociology, history, philosophy, ethics, and law in health and health care.

IRE: INVESTIGATIVE REPORTERS AND EDITORS
138 Neff Annex
Columbia, MO 65211
(573) 882-2042
Fax: (573) 884-5544
http://www.ire.org

IRE's goal is to assist other investigative reporters in their pursuit of stories.

IRISH AMERICA
432 Park Ave. South
Room 1503
New York, NY 10016
(212) 725-2993
Fax: (212) 779-1198

For those Americans who seek a better understanding of the Irish in the United States.

IRISH VOICE
432 Park Ave. S., Suite 1503
New York, NY 10016
(212) 684-3366
Fax: (212) 779-1198

Provides news and information of Irish American concern.

IRONWORKER
1750 New York Ave. NW
Suite 700
Washington, DC 20006
(202) 383-4800
Fax: (202) 638-4856

A newsletter of the Iron Workers Union.

ISSUES IN SCIENCE AND TECHNOLOGY
1636 Hobart St. NW
Washington, DC 20009
(202) 965-5648
Fax: (202) 965-5649
kfinnera@nas.edu
http://www.nas.edu

A journal that covers all areas of science, technology, health, and related policy issues in the United States.

IUE NEWS
1126 16th St. NW
Washington, DC 20036
(202) 785-7200
Fax: (202) 785-4563
info@iue.org
http://www.iue.org

An official publication of the International Union of Elecronic, Electrical, Salaried, Machine and Furniture Workers, AFL-CIO.

JEWISH TELEGRAPHIC AGENCY
330 Seventh Ave.
New York, NY 10001-5010
(212) 643-1890

Fax: (212) 643-8498

Information about the lives, fate, and well-being of Jews of all countries and serves as a link among the various Jewish communities world-wide.

JEWISH WEEK, THE
1501 Broadway, Suite 505
New York, NY 10036
(212) 921-7822
http://www.jta.org

In seeking to build and strengthen Jewish community while championing an aggressive and independent press.

JOURNAL OF BLACKS IN HIGHER EDUCATION, THE
200 West 57th St.
15th floor
New York, NY 10019
(212) 399-1084
Fax: (212) 245-1973
info@jbae.com

Higher education journal on Black Americans.

JOURNAL OF COMMUNITY PRACTICE
School of Social Work
CB #3550
Chapel Hill, NC 27599
(800) 342-0678
Fax: (800) 895-0582

A journal of organizing, planning, development, and change.

JOURNAL OF PESTICIDE REFORM
P.O. Box 1393
Eugene, OR 97440
(541) 344-5044
Fax: (541) 344-6923
info@pesticide.org
http://www.efn.org/~ncap

Dedicated to prevention of pest problems and the use of alternatives to pesticides.

JOURNAL OF PRISONERS ON PRISONS
P.O. Box 54
University Centre
Winnipeg, MB R3T 2N2
Canada
http://www.synapse.net/
~arrakis/jpp/jpp.html

A journal composed of contributions by prisoners and former prisoners.

JOURNALISM AND MASS COMMUNICATION QUARTERLY
National Center for Communication Studies
George Washington Univ.
Washington, DC 20052
(204) 994-6226
Fax: (212) 994-5806
aejmc@scu.edu
http://www.aejmc.sc.edu

A scientific research publication about journalism and mass communication.

THE KEYSTONE
A Publication of Pennsylvania
Coalition of Citizens with
Disabilities
101 S. Second Street
Suite 4
Harrisburg, PA 17101
(717) 238-0172
TTY: (717) 238-3433
josbyz@aol.com or
jbpccd@aol.com

This 'zine exposes the truth
of what life is really like for
people with disabilities,
including what our government doesn't want you to
know. Written from the
Disabled community's
perspective, it is a unique
mixture of news articles and
culture, ranging in style from
rabid to folksy.

KICK IT OVER
P.O. Box 5811, Station A
Toronto, ON M5W 1P2
Canada

Advocating Anarchism as a
form of social organization
based on personal responsibil-
ity and mutual co-operation.

KINESIS
#301-1720 Grant St.
Vancouver, B.C. V6A 2G2
Canada
(604) 255-5499
Fax: (604) 255-5511
Kinesis@wes.net
http://www.web.net/kinesis

A journal of news, features,
art reviews, commentary of
and for women to work
actively for social change.

KOREA TIMES
4525 Wilshire Boulevard
Los Angeles, CA 90010
(213) 692-2043
Fax: (213) 738-1103
http://www.koreatimela.com

A monthly bilingual
publication for reaching
Korean families in the
United States as a family
journal for parents and their
children.

LABOR NEWS FOR
WORKING FAMILIES, I.I.R.
2521 Channing Way, #5555
Berkeley, CA 94720
(510) 643-6814
Fax: (510) 642-6432
http://socrates.berkeley.edu/
    laborproject.berkeley.edu

Highlights union policies and
benefits including family
leave, child care, elder care,
flexible work.

LABOR NOTES
7435 Michigan Ave.
Detroit, MI 48210
(313) 842-6262
Fax: (313) 842-0227
labornotes@labornotes.org

Focuses on news and
information for workplace
activists.

LABORATORY MEDICINE
2100 West Harrison St.
Chicago, IL 60612
(312) 738-1336
Fax: (312) 738-0101
labmed@ascp.org
http://www.ascp.org

A newsletter of ASCP, a
not-for-profit medical society
organized exclusively for
educational, scientific, and
charitable purposes.

LAMBDA BOOK REPORT
P.O. Box 73910
Washington, DC 20056
(202) 462-7924
Fax: (202) 462-5264
LBREditor@aol.com
http://www.lambda.lit.org

Trade news publishing
information for gay and
lesbian writers.

LAPIS MAGAZINE
83 Spring St.
New York, NY 10012
(212) 334-0210
Fax: (212) 219-1347
NYOC@aol.com

Addresses both the inner
world of soul and spirit and
the outer world of politics,
society, and ecology.

LATIN AMERICAN
PERSPECTIVES
1150 University, Suite 107
Riverside, CA 92517
(909) 787-1571

Fax: (909) 787-5685

An academic journal on Latin
American issues.

LEFT BUSINESS OBSERVER
250 West 85th St.
New York, NY 10024-3217
(212) 874-4020
Fax: (212) 874-3137
dhenwood@panix.com
A journal of news and
analysis.

LEFT CURVE
P.O. Box 472
Oakland, CA 94604
(510) 763-7193
leftcurve@wco.com
http://www.ncal.verio.com/
~leftcurv

An artist-produced magazine
addressing problems of
cultural forms emerging from
problems of modernity.

LEGAL TIMES
1730 M St. NW
Suite 802
Washington, DC 20036
(202) 457-0686
Fax: (202) 457-0718
legaltimes@legaltimes.com
http://www.american
lawyer.com

A weekly legal newspaper.

LIBERTY
55 West Oak Ridge Dr.
Hagerstown, MD 21740
(301) 791-7000

A magazine of religious freedom.

LIBRARIANS AT LIBERTY
1716 SW Williston Road
Gainesville, FL 32608
(352) 335-2200

Aims to give people working in libraries and related fields an unconstrained opportunity to express professional concerns.

LILITH
250 West 57th St.
New York, NY 10107
(212) 757-0818
Fax: (212) 757-5705

A full color magazine for Jewish women.

LINGUAFRANCA
22 West 38th St.
New York, NY 10018
(212) 302-0336
Fax: (212) 302-0847
edit@linguafranca.com
http://www.linguafranca.com

A magazine for anyone with an intellectual and morbid curiosity about academic goings-on.

LIP
1400 W. Devon, #243
Chicago, IL 60660
(773) 381-1993
lip@enteract.com
http://www.NETural.com/lip

Published quarterly, *LIP* provides articles and interviews on global economic and political issues, cultural criticism dealing with race and sexuality, humor, satire and fiction, as well as thoughtful reviews of new books. Includes collaborative WorldWatch news digest section produced by the Direct Action Media Network and New York Transfer News.

LITTLE INDIA
1800 Oak Lane
Reading, PA 19604
(610) 396-0366
Fax: (610) 396-0367

Monthly trenchant commentaries on overseas Indian life.

LM MAGAZINE
P.O. Box 769
Murray Hill Station
New York, NY 10156
im@informinc.co.uk
http://www.informinc.co.uk

A loud-mouthed free speech magazine which dares to publish what others are frightened to whisper.

LRA'S ECONOMIC NOTES
145 West 28th St., 6th Fl.
New York, NY 10001
(800) 875-8775
Fax: (212) 714-1674

gregt@ira.ny.com
http://www.lra/ny.com

A journal of labor, economics, and politics for labor policy makers.

LUNA MEDIA SERVICES
P.O. Box 1265
Eureka, CA 95502
(707) 839-8974
lunanews@humboldt1.com
http://www.lunatree.org

A monthly update of Julia Butterfly's one plus year sit in her heroic vigil to save the last remaining old growth redwoods of Northern California.

MASALA
87 Fifth Ave.
Suite 603
New York, NY 10003
(212) 627-2522
Fax: (212) 627-5657

A quarterly covering issues of interest to Asians and Pacific Islanders.

MEDIA BYPASS
P.O. Box 5326
Evansville, IN 47716
(812) 477-8670
Fax: (812) 477-8677
newsroom@4bypass.com
http://www.4bypass.com

A national magazine culled from alternative sources.

MEDIA REPORT
TO WOMEN
10606 Mantz Road
Silver Spring, MD 20903
(301) 445-3231
sheilagib@aol.com

Reports and commentary about the media's depiction of women and girls.

MEDIA WATCH
P.O. Box 618
Santa Cruz, CA 95061
(408) 0423-6355
Fax: (408) 423-6355
mwatch@cruzio.com
http://www.mediawatch.com

Works to challenge media bias through education and action.

MICRORADIO
EMPOWERMENT
COALITION
2-12 Seaman Ave, 5K
New York, NY 10034
212-942-8899
mec@tao.ca
http://www.radio4all.org/
    news/mec.html

Coalition building, education and action to end the twenty-one year ban on community access to the airwaves. The Coalition specifically advocates for the non-commercial legalization of microradio.

MIDDLE EAST REPORT
1500 Massachusetts Aveune,
NW, Suite 119
Washington, DC 20005
(202) 223-3677
Fax: (202) 223-3604
merip@igc.org
http://www.merip.org

A journal offering an
independent critical voice
on the Middle East.

MILITARY AND THE
ENVIRONMENT
222-B View St.
Mountain View, CA 94041
(415) 904-7751
Fax: (415) 904-7765
cpro@igc.apc.org

Aimed at educating the public
about current issues and
legislation related to the
military and its impact on
the environment.

MINORITY BUSINESS
ENTREPRENEUR (MBE)
3528 Torrance Blvd., Suite 101
Torrance, CA 90503
(310) 540-9398
Fax: (310) 792-8263

A multi-ethnic, bi-monthly
business magazine.

MOMENT
4710 41st St., NW
Washington, DC 20016
(202) 364-3300
Fax: (202) 364-2636

A bi-monthly publication
covering Jewish issues.

MONTHLY REVIEW
122 West 27th St.
New York, NY 10001
(212) 691-2555
Fax: (212) 727-3676
mreview@igc.apc.org
http://www.peacenet.org

An independent socialist
magazine.

MOTHER JONES
731 Market St.
Suite 600
San Francisco, CA 94103
(415) 665-6637
Fax: (415) 665-6696
query@motherjones.com
http://www.motherjones.com

The magazine of investigative
journalism; now with the
on-line sister "mojowire."

MOTHERING
649 Harkle Rd.
Suite F
P.O. Box 1690
Santa Fe, NM 87505
(505) 984-8116
Fax: (505) 986-8335
mother@ni.net
http://www.mothering.com

Mothering celebrates the
experience of parenthood
while offering helpful
information.

MOUTH: VOICE OF THE
DISABILITY NATION
61 Brighton St.
Rochester, NY 14607-2656
(716) 244-6599
Fax: (716) 244-9798

Mouth speaks the
unspeakable, questions the
unquestionable, follows the
money in the $100 billion
disability exploitation
industry.

MS. MAGAZINE
20 Exchange Place
22nd Fl.
New York, NY 10005
(212) 509-2092
Fax: (212) 509-24-7

The founding magazine of the
feminist movement, ad-free,
national and international
focus on issues affecting
women.

MSRRT NEWSLETTER:
Library Alternatives
4645 Columbus Ave. South
Minneapolis, MN 55407
(612) 694-8572
Fax: (612) 541-8600
cdodge@sun.hennepin.lib.
    mn.us
http://www.cs.unca.edu/
    ~davidson/msrrt

A newsletter of commentary,
news, and networking information for activist librarians
and cultural workers.

MULTINATIONAL
MONITOR
P.O. Box 19405
Washington, DC 20036
(202) 387-8034
Fax: (202) 234-5176
monitor@essential.org

A journal that tracks
corporate activity, especially
in the Third World.

NABJ JOURNAL
3100 Taliaferro Hall
University of Maryland
College Park, MD 20742
(301) 405-8500
Fax: (301) 405-8555

Publication of the National
Association of Black
Journalists, the largest media
organization of people of color
in the world.

NACLA REPORT ON
THE AMERICAS
475 Riverside Dr., Suite 454
New York, NY 10115
(212) 870-3146
Fax: (212) 870-3305
nacla@nacla.org
http://www.nacla.org

Analyzes the major political,
social and economic trends in
Latin America.

NAJA NEWS
1433 E. Franklin Ave., Suite 11
Minneapolis, MN 55404
(612) 376-0441
Fax: (612) 376-0448

A quarterly newsletter of the Native American Journalists Association.

NATION, THE
33 Irving Place
New York, NY 10003
(212) 209-5400
Fax: (212)463.9712
info@thenation.com
http://www.thenation.com

America's oldest running weekly is a leading forum for leftist debate and investigative journalism. Also home of Radio Nation and The Nation Institute.

NATION, THE
P.O. Box 48036
5678 Park Ave.
Montreal, PQ H2V 4S8
Canada
(514) 272-3077
Fax: (514) 278-9914
beesum@odyssee.net
http://www.beesum-commu
    nication.com

We provide indigenous people in the north with a bi-monthly magazine.

NATIONAL CAMPAIGN FOR FREEDOM OF EXPRESSION QUARTERLY
918 'F' St. NW, #609
Washington, DC 20004
(800) 477-6233; (202) 393-2787
Fax: (202) 347-7376

ncfe@artswire.org
http://www.artswire.org/
    ~ncfe

An educational and advocacy magazine for artists, arts organizations, audience members, and concerned citizens for fighting censorship.

NATIONAL CATHOLIC REPORTER
P.O. Box 419281
Kansas City, MO 64141
(816) 531-0538
Fax: (816) 968-2280
lesliewirp@aol.com
http://www.natcath.com

An independent, catholic newsweekly covering events related to the church.

NATIONAL GREEN PAGES
1612 K St. NW
Suite 600
Washington, DC 20006
(800) 58-GREEN
(202) 872-5307
Fax: (202) 331-8166
info@coopamerica.org
http://www.greenpages.org

A directory of thousands of responsible businesses, products, and services published yearly.

NATIONAL MINORITY
POLITICS
13555 Bammel N. Houston
#227
Houston, TX 77066
(281) 444-4265
Fax: (281) 583-9534

A monthly publication by and
about African-Americans and
Hispanics with a conservative
political bent.

NATIONAL REVIEW
150 East 35th St.
New York, NY 10016
(212) 679-7330
Fax: (212) 696-0309
http://www.national
   review.com

Opinion and commentary
from a conservative
perspective.

NATIVE AMERICAS:
Akwekon's Journal of
Indigenous Issues
Cornell University
300 Caldwell Hall
Ithaca, NY 14853
(607) 255-4308
Fax: (607) 255-0185
mac3@cornell.edu, jeb23@
   cornell.edu,
or bfwz@cornell.edu
http://nativeamericas.aip.
   cornell.edu/

Covers the most important
and critical issues of concern
to Native peoples throughout
the Western Hemisphere.

NEA TODAY
1201 16th St. NW
Washington, DC 20036
(202) 822-7207
Fax: (202) 822-7206
NEAToday@aol.com
http://www.neatoday.com

Provides insights on
educational challenges
facing the U.S. today.

NEIGHBORHOOD
WORKS, THE
2125 West North Ave.
Chicago, IL 60647
(773) 278-4800
Fax: (773) 278-3840
tnwedit@cnt.org
http://www.cnt.org/tnw/

A bimonthly magazine
that seeks out those people,
projects and issues that
demonstrate substantial
principles at work in urban
areas.

NETWORK JOURNAL,
THE
333 Nostrand Ave.
New York, NY 11216
(212) 962-3791
Fax: (718) 399-9027
http://www.tnj.com

Offers ideas in the areas of
management, marketing,
finance, office technology,
banking and taxes.

NETWORK NEWS, THE
1325 G St., NW
Washington, DC 20005
(202) 347-1140
Fax: (202) 347-1168

A bi-weekly newsletter
focusing on women's health
and related subjects.

NEW CITIZEN, THE
34 Wall St., #407
Ashville, NC 28801
(704) 255-0182
Fax: (704) 254-2286
cml@main.nc.us
http://www.main.nc.us/cml/

Links media literacy with
the concepts and practices of
citizenship—provides media
analysis and criticism.

NEW CITY MAGAZINE
P.O. Box 26083
Winnepeg, MB R3C 4K9
Canada
(204) 775-9327
Fax: (204) 788-0109

A critical forum on the modern city, New City explains
and promotes an urban ecological society.

NEW DEMOCRACY
P.O. Box 427
Boston, MA 02130
(617) 566-9637
Newdem@aol.com
http://users.aol.com/newdem

Founded to help people
in their struggle against
capitalism, to shape the
world with anti-capitalist
values of solidarity, equality,
and democracy.

NEW PARTY NEWS
88 Third Ave., Suite 313
Brooklyn, NY 11217
(718) 246-3713
Fax: (718) 246-3718
newparty@newparty.org
http://www.newparty.org

The New Party is a grass-
roots-based democratic
political party now in active
formation in a dozen states.

NEW PERSPECTIVES
QUARTERLY
10951 West Pico Blvd., 3rd Fl.
Los Angeles, CA 90064
(310) 474-0011
npq@pacificnet.ne/

Offering economic and political thought, on a global scale,
from different points of view
in a thematic format.

NEW REPUBLIC, THE
1220 19th St., NW
Washington, DC 20036
(202) 331-7494
Fax: (202) 331-0275
tnr@aol.com
http://magazines.enews.com/
    magazines/tnr

America's leading weekly
journal of political opinion.

NEW SCIENTIST
201 Spear St., Suite 400
San Francisco, CA 94105
(888) 800-8077
Fax: (202) 331-2082
newscientist@lexis-nexis
http://www.newscientist.com

Devoted to science and technology and their impact on the way we live.

NEW YORK
AMSTERDAM NEWS
2340 Frederick Douglass Blvd.
New York, NY 10027
(212) 932-7400
Fax: (212) 222-3842

Provides a unique understanding of the New York community and the country.

NEWS FROM INDIAN
COUNTRY
7831 N. Grindstone Ave.
Hayward, WI 54843-2052
(715) 634-5226
Fax: (715) 634-3243
newsfic.aol.com
http://www.journalism.wisc.
    edu/nfic

Provides national Native news and information, as well as cultural and pow-wow updates.

NEWS INDIA
244 Fifth Ave.
New York, NY 10001
(212) 481-3110
Fax: (212) 889-5774

The only four-color English-language weekly serving the million-strong Asian Indians settled in the United States.

NEWS MEDIA AND
THE LAW
1101 Wilson Blvd., Suite 1910
Arlington, VA 22209
(703) 807-2100
Fax: (703) 807-2109
http://www.rcfp.org/rcfp

A quarterly magazine which covers issues related to news reporting and the media, and the legal issues therein.

NEWS MEDIA UPDATE
1101 Wilson Blvd., Suite 1910
Arlington, VA 22209
(703) 807-2100
Fax: (703) 807-2109
http://www.rcfp.org/rcfp

A twice-monthly newsletter regarding current media issues.

NEWS ON EARTH
P.O. Box 20065
New York, NY 10011
(212) 365
Fax: (212) 979-2055
spectator@newslet.com
http://www.newslet.com/
    washingtonspectator

A politically independent newsletter that reports on the vital issues of the day and tells the real story about what is going on in Washington.

NEWSLETTER ON
INTELLECTUAL FREEDOM
50 East Huron St.
Chicago, IL 60611
(312) 280-4223
Fax: (312) 280-4227
nperez@ala.org
http://www.ala.org/oif.html

Newsletter of the ALA's
(Americian Library
Association) office of
intellectual freedom.

NEWSPAPER GUILD, THE
501 Third St. NW
Washington, DC 20001
(202) 434-7177
Fax: (202) 434-1472
http://www.newsguild.org/

This is the newsletter for the
Newspaper Guild—CWA's
(Communications Workers of
America) 30,000 members in
the U.S. and Canada.

NEWSPAPER RESEARCH
JOURNAL
Ohio University
Athens, OH 45701
(740) 593-2590
Fax: (740) 593-2592
Bridges the gap between
the newspaper industry and
academy.

NEWSPRINTS
P.O. Box 19405
Washington, DC 20036
(202) 387-8030
Fax: (202) 234-5176

newsprints@essential.org
http://www.essential.org/

Publishes leads the national
dailies and network news
shows miss.

NEWSWATCH
MONITOR
School of Communication
Simon Fraser University
8888 University Dr.
Burnaby, BC V5A 1S6
Canada
(604) 291-4905
Fax: (604) 291-4204
censored@sfu.ca

A quarterly newsletter
which reports on Canada's
media performance.

NEW TIMES
1950 Sawtelle Blvd.
Suite 200
Los Angeles, CA 90025
(310) 477-0403
Fax: (310) 478-9875
editior@newtimesla.com
http://www.newtimesla.com

A place to get the real truth
about L.A; this weekly has
taken on such topics as the
city's poor, enforcement of
anti-slum laws, horrid safety
conditions in the building
L.A.'s new metro system, and
many more alternative
issues.

NEXUS
P.O. Box 177
Kempton, IL 60946-0177
(815) 253-6464
Fax: (815) 253-6454
nexususa@earthlink.net
http://www.icom.net/~nexus/

Since Nexus recognizes that humanity is undergoing a massive transformation, it seeks to provide "hard-to-get" information so as to assist people through these changes.

NONVIOLENT
ACTIVIST, THE
339 Lafayette St.
New York, NY 10012
(212) 228-0450
Fax: (212) 228-6193
wri@igc.apc.org

Political analysis from a pacifist perspective.

NUCLEAR
MONITOR, THE
1424 16th St., NW
Suite 404
Washington, DC 20036
(202) 328-0002
Fax: (202) 462-2183
nirsnet@igc.apc.org
http://www.nirs.org

A publication of the Nuclear Information & Resource Service.

NUCLEAR
RESISTER, THE
P.O. Box 43383
Tucson, AZ 85733-3383
(520) 323-8697
nukeresister@igc.org
Information about and support for imprisoned anti-nuclear activists.

NUTRITION ACTION
HEALTHLETTER
1875 Connecticut Ave., NW
Suite 300
Washington, DC 20009-5728
(202) 332-9110
Fax: (202) 265-4954
cspi@cspinet.org
http://www.cspinet.org

Dedicated to promoting health and nutrition from a scientific, political, and public interest perspective.

OBJECTOR, THE:
A Magazine of Conscience and Resistance
955 Sutter, #514
San Francisco, CA 94102
(415) 474-3002
Fax: (415) 474-2311
cccowr@peacenet.org
http://www.libertynet.org/
    ccco/

Magazine of the Central Committee for Conscientious Objectors.

OCAW REPORTER
255 Union Blvd.
Lakewood, CO 80228-8200
(303) 987-2229
LBaker@ocaw.org
http://www.ocaw.org

Official newsletter of the
Oil, Chemical, and Atomic
Workers Union.

OFF OUR BACKS: A
Women's Newsjournal
2337-B 18th St., NW
Washington, DC 20009
(202) 234-8072
Fax: (202) 234-8092

National and international
news on feminist issues.

OKLAHOMA INDIAN
TIMES
P.O. Box 50039
Tulsa, OK 74150
(918) 747-2773
Fax: (918) 743-1238
editor@okit.com
http://www.okit.com

A leading Indian news
source for Oklahoma and
the nation.

OMB WATCHER
1742 Connecticut Ave., NW
Washington, DC 20009-1171
(202) 234-8494
Fax: (202) 234-8584
ombwatch@rtk.net
http://ombwatch.org/
    ombwatch.html

Focuses on budget issues and
activities at the Office of
Management and Budget in
Washington.

ON THE ISSUES
29-28 41st Ave.
Long Island City, NY 11101
(718) 786-5000
Fax: (718) 784-9711

A feminist, humanist
magazine of critical thinking.

ORGANIZING
5600 City Ave.
Philadelphia, PA 19131
(215) 878-4253
Fax: (215) 879-3148

Dedicated to coverage of
community organizations
who are actively participating
in local affairs.

OUR SCHOOLS/
OUR SELVES
107 Earl Grey Road
Toronto, ON M4J 3L6
Canada
(416) 463-6978
Fax: (416) 463-6978

A magazine for Canadian
education activists, providing
analysis of educational
issues and information
about activism.

OUR STRUGGLE/
NUESTRA LUCHA
Democratic Socialists
of America
P.O. Box 162394
Sacramento, CA 95816
(916) 361-9072
campsd@csus.edu
http://www.jps.net/lryder\
    index

Newsletter of Anti-Racism,
Latino, African American
Commissions.

OUR TIMES
P.O. Box 182
New Glasgow, NS B2H 5E2
Canada
(902) 755-6840
Fax: (902) 755-1292
ourstory@web.net
http://www.ourtimes.web.net

Focuses on social change
through unionism and
democratic socialism.

OUT MAGAZINE
110 Green St.
Suite 600
New York, NY 94942-10012
(212) 334-9119
Fax: (212) 334-9227
outmag@aol.com

A general interest gay and
lesbian magazine.

OUTLOOK
#3-6184 Ash St.
Vancouver, BC V5Z 3G9
Canada
(604) 324-5101
(604) 325-2470

Supports multiculturalism,
self-determination of people
all over the world.

PAPERWORKER
3340 Perimeter Hill Dr.
Nashville, TN 37202
(615) 834-8590
Fax: (615) 831-6791

Official publication of the
International Paperworkers'
Union.

PATHFINDER
P.O. Box 649
Luck, WI 54853
(715) 472-4185
Fax: (715) 472-4184
nukewatch@win.bright.net

Encourages a non-violent
change for an environment
free of the nuclear industry
and weapons of mass
destruction.

PEACE BRIGADES INTER-
NATIONAL/USA REPORT
2642 College Ave.
Berkeley, CA 94704
(510) 540-0749
Fax: (510) 849-1247
pbiusa@igc.apc.org
http://www.igc.org/pbi/
    index/html.

Provides quarterly updates to the supporters of PBI (Peace Brigades International) in the U.S. about the work of their peace teams in seven regions of the world.

PEACE MAGAZINE
736 Bathurst St.
Toronto, ON M5S 2R4
Canada
(416) 533-7581
Fax: (416) 531-6214
mspencer@web.net
http://www.peace
    magazine.org

Issues and activities of movements for peace and non-violence around the world.

PEACE REVIEW:
A Transnational Quarterly
2130 Fulton St.
San Francisco, CA 94117
(415) 422-6349; (415) 422-6496
Fax: (415) 422-2772
(415) 388-2631
eliasr@usfca.edu

Focusing on the current issues that underlie the promotion of a more peaceful earth.

PEACEWORK
2161 Massachusetts Ave.
Cambridge, MA 02140
(617) 661-6130
Fax: (617) 354-2832
pwork@igc.apc.org

Intended to serve the movements for non-violent social change, particularly in the Northeast.

PERMACULTURE
ACTIVIST, THE
P.O. Box 1209
Black Mountain, NC 85034
(828) 298-2812
Fax: (828) 298-6441
pcactivist@mindspring.com

Advocates and documents ecological design of housing, landscapes and settlements.

POCLAD: PROGRAM
ON CORPORATIONS,
LAW & DEMOCRACY
P.O. Box 246 S.
Yarmouth, MA 02664-0246
(508) 398-1145
Fax: (508) 398-1552
people@poclad.org

A quarterly publication that instigates democratic conversations and actions that contest the authority of corporations to govern.

POLISH-AMERICAN
JOURNAL
1275 Harlem Road
Buffalo, NY 14206
(716) 893-5771
Fax: (716) 893-5783

Dedicated to the preservation and continuance of Polish American culture in the United States.

PORTLAND SKANNER
2337 North Williams Ave.
or P.O. Box 5455
Portland, OR 97227
(503) 287-3562
(800) 755-COPYT

Takes on hard issues affecting
Blacks and other minorities,
and offers positive role mod-
els for youth—stories not usually covered by the media.

POZ MAGAZINE
1279 Old Chelsea Station
New York, NY 10113-1279
(212) 242-2163
Fax: (212) 675-8505
edit@poz.com
http://www.poz.com

Focusing on quality of life
issues for anyone impacted
by AIDS and HIV.

PR WATCH
3318 Gregory St.
Madison, WI 53711
(608) 233-3346
Fax: (608) 238-2236
stauber@compuserve.com
http://www.prwatch.org

Investigates corporate and
government propoganda.
The editors also wrote *Toxic
Sludge is Good For You: Lies,
Damn Lies and the Public
Relations Industry.*

PRAYING
P.O. Box 419335
Kansas City, MO 64141
(800) 333-7373 or
(816) 531-0538

Spirituality for everday
listening—published 8
times a year.

PREVAILING WINDS
MAGAZINE
P.O. Box 23511
Santa Barbara, CA 93121
(805) 899-3433
Fax: (805) 899-4773
patrick@silcom.com
http://www.prevailing
    winds.org

Devoted to exposing
assassination, political
scandals, medical fraud,
crime, media manipulation,
corruption, mind control,
and high strangeness.

PRINCETON
PROGRESSIVE REVIEW
315 West College
Princeton, NJ 08544
progrev@princeton.edu
http://www.princeton.edu/
    ~progrev

A journal of news analysis
and occasional cultural
critique, voicing social justice
—Subscriptions are on-line.

PRISON LEGAL NEWS
2400 NW 80th St.
Suite 148
Seattle, WA 98117
(206) 781-6524
pwright@prisonlegalnews.org
http://www.prisonlegalnews.
org

Reports court rulings
involving prisoner's rights
as well as providing news
and commentary on criminal
justice issues.

PROBE
139 W. 13th St., #6
New York, NY 10011-7856
(212) 647-0200
Fax: (212) 463-8002
http://probenewsletter.com

Investigative and interpretive
newsletter promoting science
and rationality as key
elements in a democratic
society.

PROGRESSIVE LIBRARIAN
P.O. Box 2203
Times Square Station
New York, NY 10108
(973) 623-7642
http://www.libr.org

A journal for critical studies
and progressive politics.

PROGRESSIVE
POPULIST, THE
P.O. Box 150517
Austin, TX 78715-0517
(512) 447-0455

populist@usa.net
http://www.populist.com

Promotes the idea that people
are more important than corporations.

PROGRESSIVE
REVIEW, THE
1739 Connecticut Ave, NW
Washington, DC 20009-8922
(202) 232-5544
Fax: (202) 234-6222
editor@prorev.com
http://www.prorev.com

Hard-hitting reporting, good
writing, thought-provoking
agument, and wit. It grew out
of the underground press of
the 1960s to become the
capital's resident maverick.

PROGRESSIVE, THE
409 East Main St.
Madison, WI 53703
(608) 257-4626
Fax: (608) 257-3373
progressive@peacenet.org
http://www.progressive.org

Discusses peace, politics,
social justice, and
environmental concerns
from a liberal point of view.

PROMETHEUS RADIO
PROJECT
(212) 946-5251
prp@tao.ca
http://prometheus.tao.ca/

A not-for-profit association dedicated to the democratization of the airwaves through the proliferation of non-commercial, community based, micropower stations. It is our belief that access to communications for all citizens is at the heart of a democratic society.

PROUT JOURNAL, THE
P.O. Box 56466
Washington, DC 20040
(202) 829-2278
Fax: (202) 829-0462
proutwdc@igc.org
http://www.prout.org

A forum for linking spirituality and social issues.

PUBLIC CITIZEN MAGAZINE
1600 20th St., NW
Washington, DC 20009
(202) 588-1000
Fax: (202) 588-7799
pnye@citizen.org
http://www.citizen.org

Consumer rights, safety issues, corporate and business accountability, environmental issues, and citizen empowerment.

PUBLIC EYE, THE
120 Beacon St., Suite 202
Somerville, MA 02143-4304
(617) 661-9313
Fax: (617) 661-0059

publiceye@igc.apc.org
http://www.publiceye.org/pra/

A quarterly newsletter featuring an in-depth analysis and critique of issues pertaining to the U.S. political right wing.

QUE PASA
P.O. Box 65097
Toronto, ON M4K 3Z2
Canada
(416) 423-1340
Fax: (416) 423-1340

The only Toronto magazine written in English focusing on Hispanic culture.

QUILL
16 South Jackson St.
or P.O. Box 77
Greencastle, IN 46135-0077
(765) 653-3333
Fax: (765) 653-4631
spj@spjhq.org
http://www.spj.org

A national magazine that reports on journalism.
RACHEL'S ENVIRONMENT & HEALTH WEEKLY
P.O. Box 5036
Annapolis, MD 21403-7036
(410) 263-1584
Fax: (410) 263-8944
erf@rachel.clark.net

Reports on medical and scientific studies linking environment and health.

RADIANCE: The Magazine
for Large Women
P.O. Box 30246
Oakland, CA 94604
(510) 482-0680
info@radiancemagazine.com
http://www.radiance
    magazine.com

An upbeat, positive,
empowering, quarterly
magazine for women all
sizes of large. Features in
depth interviews with plus-
size celebrities, along with
up-to-date articles on health,
media, fashion, and politics.
Encourages and supports
readers in living proud, full,
active lives, now, with self-
love and self-respect.

RADICAL AMERICA
237-A Holland
Somerville, MA 02144
(617) 628-6585
Fax: (617) 628-6585

Publication of the Alternative
Education Project.

RAISE THE STAKES: The
Planet Drum Review
P.O. Box 31251
San Francisco, CA 94131
(415) 285-6556
Fax: (415) 285-6563
planetdrum@igc.org

A bi-annual review on issues
of restoration ecology and the
greening of cities.

REAPPRAISING AIDS
7514 Girard Ave., #1-331
La Jolla, CA 92037
(810) 772-9926
Fax: (619) 272-1621
philpott@wwnet.com
http://www.wwnet.com/
    ~philpott/ReappraisingAIDS

Scrutinizes the AIDS virus
from an alternative and
sometimes controversial
perspective.

REASON
3415 South Sepulveda Blvd.
Suite 400
Los Angeles, CA 90034
(310) 391-2245
Fax: (310) 390-8986
http://www.reason.com

Reports on public policy and
culture from a Libertarian
perspective.

RED STICKS PRESS
P.O. Box 59
St. Peterburg, FL 33731-0059
(813) 821-6604
Fax: (813) 821-8804
Mission is to improve
communications among
Native Americans and other
Indigenous peoples as well
as communication between
Indigenous people and the
general public.

RELIGION WATCH
P.O. Box 652
North Bellmore, NY 11710
(516) 785-6765
relwatch1@aol.com
http://www.religion
    watch.com

A monthly newsletter which
monitors trends in contemporary religion.

RESPONSIVE
PHILANTHROPY
2001 S St., NW, Suite 620
Washington, DC 20009
(202) 387-9177
Fax: (202) 332-5084
info@ncrp.org
http://www.ncrp.org

Committed to making
philanthropy more responsive
to socially, economically and
politically disenfranchised
people.

RETHINKING SCHOOLS:
An Activist Educational
Journal.
1001 E. Keefe Ave.,
Milwaukee, WI 53212
(414) 964-9646
(800) 669-4192
Fax:: (414) 964-7220
RSBusiness@aol.com
http://www.rethinkingschools.
    org

Focuses on K-12 school
reform, with an emphasis on
issues of equity and social
justice.

REVOLUTIONARY
WORKER
Box 3486
Merchandise Mart
Chicago, IL 60654
(773) 227-4066
Fax: (773) 227-4097
http://www.mcs.net/~rwor

The weekly newspaper of the
Revolutionary Communist
Party, USA.

RFD: A Journal For
Gay Men Everywhere
P.O. Box 68
Liberty, TN 37095
(615) 536-5176

A reader-written journal for
gay men focusing on country
living, and encouraging
alternative lifestyles.

RIGHTS
666 Broadway
7th Floor
New York, NY 10012
(212) 614-6464
Fax: (212) 614-6499

Covers issues involving
freedoms guaranteed by the
Constitution and Bill of
Rights.

RUSSIAN LIFE
89 Main St., #2
Montpelier, VT 05602
(802) 223-4955
Fax: (802) 223-6105

A 32 page color monthly magazine, full of fascinating stories of Russian culture, history and life in the world's largest country.

RYERSON REVIEW
OF JOURNALISM
350 Victoria St.
Toronto, Ontario M5B 2K3
Canada
(416) 979-5000 x7434
Fax: (416) 979-4216
http://www.acs.ryerson.ca

A progressive review from Ryerson Polytechnic University in Canada.

S.O.A. WATCH
(Washington)
P.O. Box 4566
Washington, DC 20017
(202) 234-3440
Fax: (202) 234-3440
http://www.derechos.org/
   soaw/

Tracks and reports on activities at the School of the Americas.

SCANDINAVIAN PRESS/
SWEDISH PRESS
1294 West 7th Ave.
Vancouver, BC V6H 1B6
Canada
(604) 731-6381
Fax: (604) 731-2292

Quarterly publication designed to provide up-to-date information from Denmark, Finland, Iceland, Norway and Sweden.

SECRECY &
GOVERNMENT BULLETIN
307 Massachusetts Ave., NE
Wahington, DC 20002
(202) 675-1012
Fax: (202) 675-1010
saftergood@igc.apc.org
http://www.fas.org/sgp/

Reports on new developments in government secrecy policies.

SE JOURNAL
P.O. Box 27280
Philadelphia, PA 19118-0280
(215) 836-9970
Fax: (215) 836-9972
SEJoffice@aol.com
http://www.sej.org

Written primarily by journalists for journalists on covering environmental issues.

SHELTERFORCE
MAGAZINE
Published by the National Housing Institute
Editor: Harold Simon
439 Main St., Suite 311
Orange, NJ 07050-1523
(973) 678-9060
Fax: (973) 678-8437
http://www.nhi.org

Covers community development and community building. Policy, theory, and on-the-ground practitioners' stories linking practitioners, policymakers, and funders, and academics.

SOCIAL JUSTICE ACTION
QUARTERLY
430 Keap St.
Brooklyn, NY 11211
(718) 218-7005
johnpotash@hotmail.com

Activist social work newspaper promoting organizing and mobilizing for social equity.

SOCIALIST WORKER
P.O. Box 339, Station E
Totonto, ON M6M 4E3
Canada
(416) 972-6391
Fax: (416) 972-6319
sworker@web.apc.org

News and analysis every two weeks of issues crucial to working Canadians.

SOCIAL POLICY
MAGAZINE
25 West 43rd St., Room 620
New York, NY 10036
(212) 642-2929
Fax: (212) 642-1956
socpol@igc.apc.org
http://www.socialpolicy.org

A quarterly magazine about progressive social change movements.

SOJOURNERS
2401 15th St., NW
Washington, DC 20009
(202) 328-8842
Fax: (202) 328-8757
sojourners@sojourners.com
http://www.sojourners.com/
    sojourners

A grassroots network for personal, community, and political transformation rooted in prophetic biblical tradition.

SOLIDARITY
8000 E. Jefferson
Detroit, MI 48214
(313) 926-5373
71112.363@compuserve.com
http://www.uaw.org
Official magazine of the United Auto Workers.

SOUTH ASIA TIMES
38 Westland Ave., Suite 23
Boston, MA 02115
(617) 536-4606
Fax: (617) 536-4606

News and views on South Asia upholding the causes of democracy, human rights, freedom of speech, disarmament and world peace.

SOUTHERN AFRICA
REPORT
603 1/2 Parliament St.
Toronto, ON M4X 1P9
Canada
(416) 967-5562
Fax: (416) 978-1547
tclsac@web.net

In-depth analysis of events
in Southern Africa.

SOUTHERN EXPOSURE
P.O. Box 531
Durham, NC 27702
(919) 419-8311 x26
Fax: (919) 419-8315
Southern@igc.apc.org

Award-winning magazine
focused on fighting for a
better South.

SPACE AND
SECURITY NEWS
5115 S. A1A Hwy.
Suite 201
Melbourne Beach, FL 32951
(407) 952-0601
ssn@rmbowman.com
http://www.rmbowan.com

Covers programs and policy
issues related to space and
space exploration.

SPIN
205 Lexington Ave
New York, NY 10016
(212) 633-8200
Fax: (212) 633-9041
spinonline@aol.com

News, issues, and profiles in
alternative music.

SPIRIT OF CRAZY HORSE
P.O. Box 583
Lawerence, KS 66044
(785) 842-5774
Fax: (785) 842-5796
lpdc@idir.net

Statements from and updates
on Leonard Peltier's case—
also focuses on native sover-
eignty and prison issues.

SPOTLIGHT, THE
300 Independence Ave., SE
Washington, DC 20003
(202) 544-1794
libertylob@aol.com
http://www.spotlight.org

News and commentary
from an ultra-conservative
perspective.

ST. LOUIS JOURNALISM
REVIEW
8380 Olive Boulevard
St. Louis, MO 63132
(314) 991-1699
Fax: (314) 997-1898

Primarily critiques what is
ignored by the local media—
also covers some national and
international news.

STAY FREE!
P.O. Box 306
New York, NY 10012
(718) 398-9324
Fax: (212) 477-5074

stayfree@sunsite.unc.edu
http://sunsite.unc.edu/
    stayfree

A magazine which casts a
critical eye on commercial-
ism and pop culture.

STEELABOR
Five Gateway Center
Pittsburgh, PA 15222
(412) 562-2442
Fax: (412) 562-2445

News & commentary of
political, economic, and social
concern to steelworkers.

STUDENT PRESS LAW
CENTER REPORT
1101 Wilson Blvd., Suite 1910
Arlington, VA 22901
(703) 807-1904
Fax: (703) 807-2109
splc@splc.org
http://www.splc.org

Reports on cases, controver-
sies, and legislation relating
to free press rights of student
journalists.

SUN, THE
107 North Roberson St.
Chapel Hill, NC 27516
(919) 942-5282

A monthly alternative literary
magazine of essays, interviews, fiction, poetry, and
photographs.

SUSTAINABLE TIMES, THE
1657 Barrington St., Suite 508
Halifax, NS B3J 2A1
Canada
(902) 423-6709
Fax: (902) 423-9736

Solutions to employment,
environment and global
development challenges.

SYNTHESIS/
REGENERATION:
A Magazine of Green
Social Thought
P.O. Box 24115
St. Louis, MO 63130
(314) 727-8554 Call first
fitzdon@aol.com

A tri-annual magazine
focusing on the social aspects
of environmentalism.

TASK FORCE
CONNECTIONS
973 Market St., Suite 600
San Francisco, CA 94103
(415) 356-8110
Fax: (415) 356-8138

Updates and reports on issues
related to AIDS prevention
and treatment.

TEACHING TOLERANCE
MAGAZINE
400 Washington Ave.
Montgomery, AL 36104
(334) 264-0286
Fax: (334) 264-3121
http://www.splcenter.org

A twice-yearly magazine covering issues related to the Teaching Tolerance Project begun by Morris Dees at the Southern Poverty Law Center.

TEAMSTER MAGAZINE
25 Louisiana Ave., NW
Washington, DC 20001
(202) 624-6911
Fax: (202) 624-6918
ibtcomm@aol.com
http://www.teamster.org

A magazine which focuses on fighting for the future and the rights of working families.

TEEN VOICES MAGAZINE
P.O. Box 120-027
Boston, MA 02112-0027
(617) 426-5505
Fax: (617) 426-5577
womenexp@teenvoices.com
http://www.teenvoices.com

A magazine that provides an interactive, educational forum that challenges media images of young women and girls.

TELEMEDIUM, THE JOURNAL OF MEDIA LITERACY
120 E. Wilson St.
Madison, WI 53703
(608) 257-7712
Fax: (608) 257-7714

Addresses issues of media literacy in the United States.

TERRAIN
2530 San Pablo Ave.
Berkeley, CA 94702
(510) 548-2235
Fax: (510) 548-2240
terrain@ecologycenter.org
http://www.ecologycenter.org

A quarterly magazine focusing on environmental issues.

THIRD FORCE
1218 East 21st St.
Oakland, CA 94606-9950
(510) 533-7583
Fax: (510) 533-0923
ctwo@igc.org

Reports on labor, low income issues, communities of color, and community activism and organizing.

THIS MAGAZINE
396-401 W. Richmond St.
Toronto, ON M5V 3A8
Canada
(416) 979-9429
Fax: (416) 979-1143
thismag@web.net

Focuses on culture, politics, labor, and feminism in Canada and internationally.

TIBET PRESS WATCH
1825 K St., NW, Suite 520
Washington, DC 20006
(202) 785-1515
Fax: (202) 785-4343
ict@peacenet.org
http://www.savetibet.org

A magazine focusing on the current situation inside Tibet as well as the support movement within the United States.

TIKKUN
P.O. Box 1778
New York, NY 10025
(212) 864-4110
Fax: (212) 864-4137
http://www.tikkun.com

A magazine that focuses on topics of particular interest to the Jewish community, including culture, politics, and philosophy.

TOWARD FREEDOM
Box 468
Burlington, VT 05402-0468
(802) 658-2523
Fax: (802) 658-3738
Tfmag@aol.com
http://www.towardfree
   dom.com

A progressive international news, analysis and advocacy journal that helps strengthen and extend human justice and liberties.

TRADEWOMEN:
A Magazine for Women in Blue Collar Work
P.O. Box 2622
Berkeley, CA 94702
(510) 548-2099

TRANSITION
25 Francis Ave.
Van Serg Hall B11
Cambridge, MA 02138
(617) 496-2847
Fax: (617) 496-2877
transit@fas.harvard.edu

An independent publication from Harvard University.

TREATMENT REVIEW
611 Broadway, Suite 613
New York, NY 10012-2809
(800) 734-7104
Fax: (212) 260-8869
atdn@aidsnyc.org
http://www.aidsnyc.org/
   network

Provides an overview of AIDS treatments in clinical trial and newly as well as general medical teatment information.

TRICYCLE:
The Buddhist Review
92 Vandam St.
New York, NY 10013
(212) 645-1143
tricycle@well.com
http://www.tricycle.com

A non-sectarian magazine examining the juxtaposition of the dharma in western culture.

TURNING THE TIDE:
Journal of Anti-Racist
Activism, Research &
Education
P.O. Box 1055
Culver City, CA 90232
(310) 288-5003
part2001@usa.net
http://www.igc.apc.org/srf

A publication from People
Against Racist Terror which
covers the direct action
movement to combat
organized white supremacist
and fascist groups, as well
as anti-colonial struggles,
political prisoner and prison
rights issues. It also exposes
links between racists, the
Christian right and state
repression.

TYNDALL WEEKLY
REPORT
135 Rivington St.
New York, NY 10002
(212) 674-8913
Fax: (212) 979-7304

A weekly fax-sheet monitor-
ing the television networks'
nightly newscasts.

U: The National
College Magazine
1800 Century Park East, #820
Los Angeles, CA 90067-1503
(310) 551-1381
Fax: (310) 551-1659
editor@umagazine.com
http://www.umagazine.com

Economic and political views
from a global perspective.

UKRAINIAN WEEKLY, THE
30 Montgomery St.
Jersey City, NJ 07302
(201) 434-0237
Fax: (201) 451-5486

For people of Ukrainian
descent and culture.

UPPNET NEWS
321 19th Ave. S., Suite 3-300
Minneapolis, MN 55455
(612) 624-4326
uppnet@labornet.org or
jsee@csom.umn.edu

Official publication of
the Union Producers and
Programmers Network,
promoting tv and radio shows
pertinent to the cause of
organized labor and working
people.

URBAN ECOLOGIST
QUARTERLY, THE
405 14th St., Suite 900
Oakland, CA 94612
(510) 251-6330
Fax: (510) 251-2117
urbanecology@urbane
  cology.org
http://www.urbanecology.org

A magazine dedicated to
creating ecologically and
socially healthy communities
—highlights examples from
throughout the world.

URGENT ACTION
NEWSLETTER
P.O. Box 1270
Nederland, CO 80466-1270
(303) 440-0913
Fax: (303) 258-7881
sharris@igc.apc.org
http://www.amnesty-usa.org

The newsletter for Amnesty
International out of the
Urgent Action Program
Office.

U.S. BLACK ENGINEER
AND INFORMATION
TECHNOLOGY
729 East Pratt St., Suite 504
Baltimore, MD 21202
(410) 244-7101
Fax: (410) 752-1837
ccgmag@aol.com
http://www.ccgmag.com

Quarterly dedicated to promoting opportunities for
Black Americans in science
and technology.

UTNE READER
1624 Harmon Place, Suite 330
Minneapolis, MN 55403
(612) 338-5040
Fax: (612)338-6043
info@utne.com
http://www.utne.com

A digest of innovative ideas
and material reprinted from
alternative and independent
media sources.

VETERAN, THE
1224 M, NW
Washington, DC 20005
(202) 628-2700
Fax: (202) 628-5880
http://www.vva.org

The official voice of Vietnam
Veterans of America.

VIBE
205 Lexington Ave., 3rd Fl.
New York, NY 10016
(212) 448-7300
Fax: (212)522-4578
http://www.vibe.com

Provides news and features
about goings-on in urban
culture.

VILLAGE VOICE
36 Cooper Square
New York, NY 10003
(212) 475-3300
Fax: (212) 475-8944
editor@villagevoice.com
http://www.villagevoice.com

A weekly newspaper covering
regional, national, and
nternational affairs from a
New York perspective.

VIVA LA TORTUGA
P.O. Box 400
Forest Knolls, CA 94933
(415) 488-0370
Fax: (415) 488-0372
seaturtles@earthisland.org

Newsletter of the Sea Turtle
Restoration Project.

VOCES DE LA FRONTERA
c/o Christina Neumann Ortiz
Pueblos Unidos building
2211-A Hildalgo St.
Austin, TX 78702

Community newspaper for
immigrants and maquiladora
workers.

WAR AND PEACE DIGEST
32 Union Square East
New York, NY 10003-3295
(212) 777-6626
Fax: (212) 777-2552
warpeace@interport.net
http://www.warpeace.org

An anti-nuclear publication
promoting peace, social justice, and media reform.

WASHINGTON
MONTHLY, THE
1611 Connecticut Ave., NW
Washington, DC 20009
(202) 462-0128
Fax: (202) 332-8413

National opinion magazine
covering politics, media, and
government.

WASHINGTON
SPECTATOR, THE
P.O. Box 20065
London Terrace Station
New York, NY 10011
(212) 741-2365
spectator@newslet.com
A twice-monthly commen-
tary on national politics.

WE INTERNATIONAL
736 Bathurst St.
Toronto, Ontario M5S 2R4
Canada
(416) 516-2600
Fax: (416) 531-6214
weed@web.net
http://www.web.net/~weed/

A magazine that examines
women's multiple relation-
ships with their environment.

WEEKLY NEWS UPDATE
ON THE AMERICAS
339 Lafayette St.
New York, NY 10012
(212) 674-9499
Fax: (212) 674-9139
wnu@igc.org
http://home.earthlink.net/
 ~dbwilson/wnuhome.html

Produces a weekly news
summary on Latin America
and the Caribbean with an
emphasis on sources from the
region and on news played
down or ignored by the U.S.
corporate media.

WELFARE MOTHERS
VOICE
2711 W. Michigan
Milwaukee, WI 53208
(414) 342-6662
Fax: (414) 342-6667

WMV provides a voice to
mothers in poverty who
receive or have received
public support for children.

WHISPERING WIND
53196 Old Uneedus Road
P.O. Box 1390
Folsom, LA 70437-1390
(504) 796-5433
Fax: (504) 796-9236

A bi-monthly magazine dedicated to preserving the traditions of the American Indian both past and present.

WHO CARES MAGAZINE
511 K St. NW, Suite 1042
Washington, DC 20005
(202) 628-1691
Fax: (202) 628-2063
info@whocares.mag
http://www.whocares.org

A national bi-monthly journal of service and action, it publishes information to help people create, grow and manage organizations for the benefit of the common good, and to foster a sense of community among social entrepeneurs nationwide.

WHOLE EARTH
MAGAZINE
1408 Mission Ave.
San Rafael, CA 94901
(415) 256-2800
Fax: (415) 256-2808
wer@well.com

Provides access to tools, ideas, and practice—reviews books and products to help people help themselves—publishes a catalogue.

WHY MAGAZINE
505 Eighth Ave., 21st Fl.
New York, NY 10018
(212) 629-8850
Fax: (212) 465-9274

A quarterly publication that challenges the existance of hunger and poverty, presenting leading thinkers and activists with information, insight, and opportunities for involvement.

WINDSPEAKER
15001-112 Ave.
Edmonton, AB T5M 2V6
Canada
(403) 455-2700
Fax: (403) 455-7639

Objective reporting of news and events that affect Canada's Aboriginal people.

WOMEN &
ENVIRONMENTS
736 Bathurst St.
Toronto, ON M5S 2R4
Canada
(416) 516-2600
Fax: (416) 531-6214
weed@web.apc.org
http://www.web.apc.org/
~weed

A look at how women interact, progress, challange and harmonize within multiple environments.

WOMEN'S EDUCATION
DES FEMMES
47 Main St.
Toronto, ON M4E 2V6
Canada
(416) 699-1909
Fax: (416) 699-2145
cclow@web.apc.org

Publication focusing on issues related to women in higher education.

WOMEN'S HEALTH
LETTER
2245 E. Colorado Blvd., # 104
Pasadena, CA 91107-3651
(626) 798-0638
Fax: (626) 798-0639

The thinking woman's guide to wellness: offers sane and sound health and healing insights.

WOMEN'S REVIEW
OF BOOKS
Wellesley College
Wellesley, MA 02181
(781) 283-2555
Fax: (781) 283-3645
lgardiner@wellesley.edu

Reviews books by and about women, in all areas including fiction, non-fiction and poetry.

WORKBOOK, THE
P.O. Box 4524
105 Stanford, SE
Albuquerque, NM 87106
(505) 262-1862
Fax: (505) 262-1864

Helps people gain access to vital information that can help them assert control over their lives.

WORLD POLICY JOURNAL
65 Fifth Ave., Suite 413
New York, NY 10003
(212) 229-5808
Fax: (212) 229-5579
robertsa@newschool.edu
http://worldpolicy.org

A leading quarterly magazine covering international affairs in the United States.

WORLD PRESS REVIEW
200 Madison Ave., Suite 2104
New York, NY 10016
(212) 982-8880
worldpress@worldpress.org
http://www.worldpress.org

A digest of the global press, a sampling of newspapers from around the world.

WORLD RIVERS REVIEW
1847 Berkeley Way
Berkeley, CA 94703
(510) 848-1155
Fax: (510) 848-1008
irn@irn.org
http://www.irn.org

Provides the latest news on the worldwide movement to stop destructive dams and information about alternatives to large hydro projects.

WORLD WATCH
1776 Massachusetts Ave., NW
Washington, DC 20036
(202) 452-1999
Fax: (202) 296-7365
www.pub@worldwatch.org
http://www.worldwatch.org

A bi-monthly publication
which informs the general
public about the damage
done by the world economy
to its environmental support
system.

WORLDVIEWS
1515 Webster, #305
Oakland, CA 94612
(510) 451-1742
Fax: (510) 835-3017
worldviews@igc.org
http://www.igc.org/
    worldviews

A quarterly review of
resources for education and
action.

YES! A Journal of Positive
Futures
P.O. Box 10818
Bainbridge Island, WA 98110
(206) 842-0216
Fax: (206) 842-5208
yes@futurenet.org
http://www.futurenet.org

A journal that helps shape
and support the evolution of
sustainable cultures and communities.

YOGA JOURNAL
2054 University Ave., Suite 600
Berkeley, CA 94704
(510) 841-9200
Fax: (510) 644-3101
info@yogajournal.com
http://www.yogajournal.com

A bi-monthly lifestyle magazine dealing with hatha yoga
and wholistic healing.

YOUTH ACTION FORUM
67 Richmond St. W., Suite 410
Toronto, ON MS4 125
Canada
(800) 718-LINK
(416) 368-2277
Fax: (416) 368-8354
695036@iran.net

A youth activist publication
dedicated to motivating and
educating young people on
the issues that are important
to them.

Z MAGAZINE
18 Millfield St.
Woods Hole, MA 02543
(508) 548-9063
lydia.sargent@lbbs.org
http://www.zmag.org/

An independent political
magazine of critical thinking
on political, cultural, social,
and economic life in the
United States. Their web
page, Z Net, is a vital
resource for movement news,
links, and daily updates.

REGIONAL PUBLICATIONS

ACE MAGAZINE
263 North Limestone St.
Lexington, KY 40507
(606) 225-4889
Fax: (606) 226-0569

ACLU NEWS
1663 Mission St.
4th Floor
San Francisco, CA 94103
(415) 621-2493

A newspaper of the American
Civil Liberties Union of
Northern California.

ARMENIAN
REPORTER, THE
P.O. Box 65060067–07
Utopia Parkway
Fresh Meadows, NY 11365
(718) 380-1200
Fax: (718) 380-8057

ASIAN PAGES
P.O. Box 11932
St. Paul, MN 55111-0932
(612) 884-3265
Fax: (612) 888-9373

ASIAN WEEK
809 Sacramento St.
San Francisco, CA 94108
(415) 397-0220
Fax: (415) 397-7258
asianweek@asianweek.com
http://www.asianweek.com

ATHENS NEWS
14 N. Court St.
Athens, OH 45701
(740) 594-8219
Fax: (740) 592-5695
anews@frognet.net

ATLANTA INQUIRER
947 M.L. King Dr., NW
Morris Brown Station
Atlanta, GA 30314
(404) 523-6086

AU-AUTHM ACTION NEWS
10005 East Osborn Road
Scottsdale, AZ 85256
(602) 850-8089
Fax: (602) 874-8064

The Pima-Maricopa Indian
Community Monthly
Newsletter.

AUSTIN CHRONICLE
P.O. Box 49066
Austin, TX 78765
(512) 454-5766
Fax: (512) 458-6910
Mail@auschron.com
http://www.auschron.com

BALTIMORE AFRO-
AMERICAN
2519 North Charles St.
Baltimore, MD 21218
(410) 554-8200
Fax: (410) 554-8213

BALTIMORE CITY PAPER
812 Park Ave.
Baltimore, MD 21201
(410) 523-2300
Fax: (410) 523-2222
letters@citypaper.com
http://www.citypaper.com

BALTIMORE JEWISH TIMES
2104 North Charles St.
Baltimore, MD 21218
(410) 752-3504
Fax: (410) 752-2375

Weekly.

BAY STATE BANNER
68 Fargo St.
Boston, MA 02210
(617) 357-4900
Fax: (617) 542-7119

African-American weekly.

BAY WINDOWS
631 Tremont St.
Boston, MA 02118
(617) 266-6670
Fax: (617) 266-6973
letters@baywindows.com
http://www.baywindows.com

BECAUSE PEOPLE
MATTER
P.O. Box 162998
Sacramento, CA 95816
(916) 444-3203
JeKeltner@aol.com

Sacramento's and the
Foothill's progressive
bi-monthly newspaper

BIG RED NEWS
155 Water St., Suite 400
Brooklyn, NY 11201
(718) 852-6001
Fax: (718) 852-7846

Weekly catering to New
York's African-Americans
and Caribbeans.

BIRMINGHAM WEEKLY
2101 Magnolia Ave. South,
4th Floor
Birmingham, AL 35205
(205) 322-2426
Fax: (205) 322-0040
sryan@bhamweekly.com

BLOOMINGTON VOICE
3900 Old South State Road
37
Bloomington, IN 47401
(812) 331-0963
Fax: (812) 337-3308
dhayes@bvoice.com
http://www.thealter
    native.com

BOISE WEEKLY
109 South 4th St.
Boise, ID 83702
(208) 344-2055
Fax: (208) 342-4733

BOSTON IRISH REPORTER
304 Neponset Ave
Dorchester, MA 02122
(617) 436-1222
Fax: (617) 825-5516

Monthly.

BOSTON PHOENIX
126 Brookline Ave.
Boston, MA 02215
(617) 450-8700
Fax: (617) 536-1463
info@phx.com
http://www.boston
    phoenix.com

BOULDER WEEKLY
690 South Lashley Lane
Boulder, CO 80303
(303) 494-5511
Fax: (303) 494-2585
bweditor@tesser.com
http://www.boulder
    weekly.com

BRIARPATCH:
Saskatchewan's Independent
News Magazine
2138 McIntyre St.
Regina, SK S4P 2R7 Canada
(306) 525-2949

Covers labor, environment,
women's rights, and politics
from a socialist perspective.

CALIFORNIA VOICE, THE
1366 Turk St.
San Francisco, CA 94115
(415) 931-5778
Fax: (415) 931-0214

African-American weekly.

CALL AND POST
(Cincinnati)
1949 E. 105th St.
Cleveland, OH 44101
(216) 791-7600

Fax: (216) 791-6568

African-American weekly.

CALL AND POST
(Cleveland)
1949 East 105th St.
Cleveland, OH 44106
(216) 791-7600
Fax: (216) 791-6568

African-American weekly.

CALL AND POST
(Columbus)
109 Hamilton Ave.
Columbus, OH 43216
(614) 224-8123
Fax: (614) 224-8517

African-American weekly.

CANYON COUNTRY
ZEPHYR, THE
P.O. Box 327
Moab, UT 84532
(435) 259-7773
zephyr@lasal.net
http://www.canyon
    countryzephyr.com

An alternative news source
serving the canyonlands area
of Utah and focusing on
environmental issues in the
area.

CAPE VERDEAN NEWS
P.O. Box 3063
New Bedford, MA 02741
(508) 997-2300
Fax: (508) 997-2300

A regional community, bi-monthly, English-language newspaper servicing the Cape Verdean-American community in southern New England.

CARIBBEAN TODAY
10730 S.W. 171 St.
Miami, FL 33157
(305) 238-2868
Fax: (305) 252-7843

Monthly.

CASCADIA TIMES
25-6 NW 23rd Place, #406
Portland, OR 97210
(503) 223-9036
Fax: (503) 736-0097
cascadia@spiritone.com
http://www.cascadia.times.org

Investigative journalism covering politics, environment, and other issues in the Pacific northwest

CASCO BAY WEEKLY
561 Congress St.
Portland, ME 04101
(207) 775-6601
Fax: (207) 775-1615
editor@cbw.maine.com
http://www.cascobay
    weekly.com

CHAR-KOOSTA NEWS
P.O. Box 278 Hwy 93 North
Pablo, MT 59855
(406) 675-3000
Fax: (406) 675-2806

Weekly local coverage of the Confederated Salish and Kootenai Tribes of the Flathead Indian Reservation.

CHEROKEE ADVOCATE
P.O. Box 948
Tahlequah, OK 74464
(918) 456-0671
Fax: (918) 456-6485

Monthly.

CHEROKEE OBSERVER
P.O. Box 1301
Jay, OK 74346-1301
(918) 253-8752
Fax: (918) 458-5381

Monthly.

CHICAGO CITIZEN
412 East 87th St.
Chicago, IL 60619
(312) 487-7700
Fax: (312) 487-7931

African-American weekly.

CHICAGO INDEPENDENT BULLETIN
2037 West 95th St.
Chicago, IL 60643
(312) 783-1040

African-American weekly.

CHICAGO INK
5706 South University Ave.
Chicago, IL 60637
(773) 955-2047
Fax: (773) 702-7718
jkw3@midway.uchicago.edu

A Chicago-wide leftist newspaper appearing monthly, focusing on Chicago media and politics.

CHICAGO LIFE
MAGAZINE
P.O. Box 11311
Chicago, IL 60611-0311
(773) 528-2737
achicagolife@mcs.com
chigolise@mcs.com

A magazine of politics, health, and environmental issues emphasizing improving quality of life.

CHICAGO NEWCITY
770 N. Halsted, Suite 208
Chicago, IL 60622
(312) 243-8786
Fax: (312) 243-8802
newcity@newcitynet.com
http://www.newcitynet.com

CHICAGO READER
11 East Illinois St.
Chicago, IL 60611
(312) 828-0350
Fax: (312) 828-0305
mail@chireader.com
http://www.chicago
    reader.com

CHICAGO WEEKEND
412 East 87th St.
Chicago, IL 60619
(312) 487-7700
Fax: (312) 487-7931

African-American weekly.

CHICO EXAMINER, THE
101 Salem St., #5
Chico, CA 95928

CHICO NEWS & REVIEW
353 E. Second St.
Chico, CA 95928
(916) 894-2300
Fax: (916) 894-0143

CINCINNATI CITIBEAT
23 East Seventh St., Suite 617
Cincinnati, OH 45202
(513) 665-4700
Fax: (513) 665-4369
letters@citybeat.com
http://www.citybeat.com

CIRCLE, THE
1530 East Franklin Ave.
Minneapolis, MN 55404
(612) 879-1760
Fax: (612) 879-1712
circlemplsa@aol.com

A monthly publication of Minneapolis-St. Paul Native American news and arts.

CITY NEWSPAPER
250 North Goodman St
Rochester, NY 14607
(716) 244-3329
Fax: (716) 244-1126
ad_dept@rochestercitynews.
    com

CITY PAGES
MINNEAPOLIS/ST. PAUL
401 N.3rd St., Suite 550
Minneapolis, MN 55401
(612) 375-1015

Fax: (612) 372-3737
letters@citypages.com
adinfo@citypages.com

CITY PAPER
812 Park Ave.
Baltimore, MD 21201
(410) 523-2300
Fax: (410) 523-8437
amarkowitz@citypaper.com
http://www.citypaper.com

CITYVIEW
100 4th St.
Des Moines, IA 50309
(515) 288-3336
Fax: (515) 288-0309
BPC@commonkink.com

CLEVELAND FREE TIMES
1846 Coventry Rd., Suite 100
Cleveland, OH 44118
(216) 321-2300
Fax: (216) 321-4456
webmaster@freetimes.com
http://www.freetimes.com

CLEVELAND JEWISH NEWS
3645 Warrensville Center Rd.
Cleveland, OH 44122-5294
(216) 991-8300
Fax: (216) 991-2088

Weekly.

COAST WEEKLY
668 Williams Ave.
Seaside, CA 93955
(408) 394-5656
Fax: (408) 394-2909
mail@coastweekly.com
http://www.coastweekly.com

COLORADO SPRINGS
INDEPENDENT
121 E. Pikes Peak, Suite 455
Colorado Springs, CO 80903
(719) 557-4545
Fax: (719) 577-4107
letters@csindy.com

COLUMBUS ALIVE
17 Brickel St.
Columbus, OH 43215
(614) 221-2449
Fax: (614) 221-2456
alive@ds.net
http://www.alivewired.com

COLUMBUS TIMES
2230 Buena Vista Road
Columbus, GA 31906
(706) 324-2404
Fax: (706) 596-0657

African-American weekly.

COMMUNIQUE
1311 Executive Center Dr.
Suite 202
Tallahassee, FL 32301-5029
(904) 877-4705
Fax: (904) 942-5798
favaca@worldnet.att.net
http://www.favaca.org

A newsletter of Florida's
unique development partnership with the Carribean.

COMMUNITY CONTACT
5151 de Maisonneuve W.
NDG
Montreal, PQ H4A 1Z3
Canada
(514) 489-4540

African-American monthly.

CONNECTIONS
P.O. Box 4123
Stockton, CA 95204
(209) 467-4455
dsteele@igc.apc.org
http://www.sonnet.com/
    usr/pjc

San Joaquin County's
alternative newspaper.

CONTEMPORA
MAGAZINE
1818 Morena St.
A.J. Cebrun Journalism
Center
Nashville, TN 37208
(615) 321-3268
Fax: (615) 321-0409

African-American quarterly.

CREATIVE LOAFING
750 Willoughby Way
Atlanta, GA 30312
(404) 688-5623
Fax: (404) 614-3599
webmaster@creative
    loafing.com
http://www.creative
    loafing.com

CREATIVE LOAFING
6112 Old Pineville Road
Charlotte, NC 28203
(704) 522-8334
Fax: (704) 522-8088
http://www.creative
    loafing.com

CURRENT, THE
3635 N. 68th St.
Scottsdale, AZ 85251
(602) 945-3544 x117
garytr@aztec.asu.edu

Bi-monthly publication
on democracy, peace, justice,
and the environment.

DALLAS OBSERVER
2130 Commerce
Dallas, TX 75201
(214) 757-9000
Fax: (214) 757-8593
http://www.dallas
    observer.com

DAYTON VOICE
1927 North Main St.
Dayton, OH 45405
(937) 275-8855
Fax: (937) 275-6056
thevoice@commkey.net

DETROIT METRO TIMES
743 Beaubien, Suite 301
Detroit, MI 48226

DETROIT SUNDAY
JOURNAL, THE
450 West Fort
Detroit, MI 48226

EAST BAY EXPRESS
931 Ashby Ave.
Berkeley, CA 94710
(510) 540-7400
Fax: (510) 540-7700
Ebxpress.@aol.com

EASY READER
832 Hermosa Ave.
Hermosa Beach, CA 90254
(310) 372-4611
Fax: (310) 318-6292

EAT THE STATE!
P.O. Box 85541
Seattle, WA 98145
ets@scn.org
http://EatTheState.org.

A weekly forum for anti-
authoritarian political opinion, research, and humor.

ECONEWS
879 Ninth St.
Arcata, CA 95521
(707) 822-6918
Fax: (707) 822-0827
nec@igc.apc.org
http://www.necandeco
   news.to

Action-oriented and timely
articles on forestry, wildlife,
toxics, recycling, energy,
endangered species, and air
and water quality in Northern
California, the Pacific
Northwest, and beyond.

EL BOHEMIO NEWS
4178 Mission St.
San Francisco, CA 94112
(415) 647-1924
Fax: (415) 824-7248

A hispanic newspaper
distributed throughout
San Francisco and the
Greater Bay Area.

EL DIARIO/LA PRENSA
143 Varick St.
New York, NY 10013
(212) 807-4600
Fax: (212) 807-4705

The voice of Latino issues
for the New York City/
tri-state area.

EL LATINO (San Diego)
P.O. Box 550
San Diego, CA 92112
(619) 299-7744
Fax: (619) 299-7743

Regional, bilingual weekly
established 1988; focused on
local Latino events.

EL MENSAJERO
346 Ninth St.
San Francisco, CA 94103
(415) 864-7612
Fax: (415) 863-6080

A Spanish language
newspaper serving the
San Francisco area with
local news coverage.

EL NUEVO HERALD
One Herald Plaza
Miami, FL 33132-1693
(305) 376-3535
Fax: (305) 376-2099

Regional daily Spanish
newspaper.

EL SOL DEL VALLE
718 North St.
Sanger, CA 93657
(209) 875-8771
Fax: (209) 875-7083

A Hispanic newspaper that serves Fresno, Madera, Tulare, and Kings Counties in California.

EL SOL DE TEXAS
4260 Spring Valley Road
Dallas, TX 75244
(214) 386-9120
Fax: (214) 386-7125

Oldest Hispanic newspaper in Dallas.

ENVIRONMENTAL
PROTECTION
INFORMATION CENTER
(EPIC)
P.O. Box 397
Garberville, CA 95542
(707) 923-2931
Fax: (707) 923-4210
epic.igc.org
http://www.igc.org/epic

EUGENE WEEKLY
1251 Lincoln
Eugene, OR 97401
(541) 484-0519
Fax: (541) 484-4044
sonjas@eugeneweekly.com
http://www.eugene
    weekly.com

EVERYBODY'S NEWS
1310 Pendleton St., Suite 700
Cincinnati, OH 45210
(513) 381-2606
Fax: (513) 287-8643

FAIRFIELD COUNTY
WEEKLY/WESTCHESTER
COUNTY WEEKLY
One Dock St.
Stamford, CT 06902
(203) 406-2406
Fax: (203) 406-1066
http://fairfieldweekly.com/
    westchesterweekly.com

FLAGPOLE MAGAZINE
112 South Foundry St.
Athens, GA 30601
(706) 549-9523
Fax: (706) 548-8981
flagpole@negia.net
http://www.flagpole.com

FOLIO WEEKLY
9456 Phillips Highway, Suite 11
Jacksonville, FL 32256
(904) 260-9770
Fax: (904) 260-9773
themail@folioweekly.com
http://www.folioweekly.com

FRONTLINES
8333 Little River Turnpike
Annandale, VA 22003
(703) 323-3579
Fax: (703) 323-3399

FW WEEKLY
1204-B W. 7th St., Suite 201
Fort Worth, TX 76102
(817) 335-9559

Fax: (817) 335-9575
pub@fwweekly.com
http://www.fwweekly.com

GAMBIT WEEKLY
3923 Bienville St.
New Orleans, LA 70119
(504) 486-5900
Fax: (504) 483-3159
http://www.bestofnew
    orleans.com

GLUE L.A.
171 Pier Ave., Suite 236
Santa Monica, CA 90405
(310) 392-1391
Fax: (310) 392-6374
gluela@aol.com
http://www.cridder.com/glue

An independent weekly
dedicated to unifying social
activism across the many
cultural, economic, and ethnic
populations in Los Angeles.

GLYPH
117 E. Louisa, #253
Seattle, WA 98102
(206) 343-5650
Fax: (206) 343-7135
Chaosunit@aol.com

Monthly tales of highbrow
pulp.

GREEN CITY
CALENDAR, THE
P.O. Box 31251
San Francisco, CA 94131
(415) 285-6556
Fax: (415) 285-6563
planetdrum@igc.org

A comprehensive listing of
bay area ecological events—
chooses a theme each
publication.

HARTFORD ADVOCATE
100 Constitution Plaza
Hartford, CT 06103
(860) 548-9300
Fax: (860) 548-9335
jreynolds@hartford
    advocate.com
http://www.hartford
    advocate.com

HEADWATERS FOREST
NEWS
84 Fourth St.
Ashland, OR 97520
(541) 482-4459
Fax: (541) 482-7282
headwtrs@mind.net
http://www.headwaters.org

HEAL ACTION MEMO
1718 W. Broadway, Suite 203
Spokane, WA 99201
(509) 326-3370
Fax: (509) 326-2932
heallfi@aol.com
http://www.iea.co,/~heal

Monthly newsletter focusing
on continuing effects of
nuclear weapons production
on health, the environment,
and the well-being of democracy—with emphasis on
issues related to the Hanford
Nuclear Plant and the Pacific
Northwest.

HISPANIC
98 San Jacinto Blvd., Suite 1150
Austin, TX 78701
(512) 476-5599

HOMELESS GAZETTE, THE
P.O. Box 1053
Dallas, TX 75221

HONOLULU WEEKLY
1200 College Walk
Honolulu, HI 96817
(808) 528-1475
Fax: (808) 528-3144
http://honoluluweekly.com

HORIZONTES
2601 Mission St., Suite 900
San Francisco, CA 94110
(415) 641-6051
Fax: (415) 282-3320

HOUR MAGAZINE
4130 Saint-Denis
Montreal, PQ H2W 25
Canada
(514) 848-0777
Fax: (514) 848-9004
http://www.afterhour.com

HOUSTON PRESS
1621 Milam, Suite 100
Houston, TX 77002
(713) 280-2400
Fax: (713) 280-2444
hfife@houstonpress.com
http://www.houstonpress.com

HYDE PARK CITIZEN
412 E. 87th St
Chicago, IL 60619
(312) 487-7700
Fax: (312) 487-7931

ICON
315 S. Dubuque
Iowa City, IA 52244
(319) 351-1531
Fax: (319) 351-0255

ILLINOIS TIMES
P.O. Box 3524
Springfield, IL 62708
(217) 753-2226
Fax: (217) 753-2281
71632.147@compuserve.com
illtimes@midwest.net

IMPACTO: The Latin News
853 Broadway, Suite 811
New York, NY 10003
(212) 505-0288
Fax: (212) 598-9414

IN PITTSBURGH
NEWSWEEKLY
2000 East Carson St.
Pittsburgh, PA 15203
(412) 488-1212
Fax: (412) 488-1217
info@inpgh.com
http://www.inpgh.com

INDEPENDENT WEEKLY
P.O. Box 2690
Durham, NC 27715
(919) 286-1972
Fax: (919) 286-4274
sioux1@mindspring.com

INDIA IN NEW YORK
43 West 24th St.
New York, NY 10010
(212) 791-3742
Fax: (212) 627-9503

INDIANAPOLIS RECORDER
2901 N. Tacoma Ave.
Indianapolis, IN 46218
(317) 924-5143
Fax: (317) 924-5148

INSIDE MAGAZINE
226 S. 16th St.
Philadelphia, PA 19102
(215) 893-5700
Fax: (215) 546-3957

A quarterly publication of the
Jewish Federation of Greater
Philadelphia.

ISTHMUS
101 King St.
Madison, WI 53703
(608) 251-5627
Fax: (608) 251-2165
edit@isthmus.com

ITALIAN VOICE, THE
P.O. Box 9
Totowa, NJ 07511-0009
(201) 942-5028
Fax: (201) 942-5028

ITHACA TIMES
P.O. Box 27
Ithaca, NY 14851
(607) 277-7000
Fax: (607) 277-1012
ithtimes@aol.com

JACKSONVILLE FREE
PRESS, THE
1603-1 W. Edgewood Ave.
Jacksonville, FL 32208
(904) 634-1993

A weekly African-American
regional.

JEWISH ADVOCATE, THE
15 School St.
Boston, MA 02108
(617) 367-9100
Fax: (617) 367-9310

JEWISH BULLETIN
225 Bush St., Suite 1480
San Francisco, CA 94104
(415) 263-7200
Fax: (415) 957-0266

JEWISH EXPONENT
226 South 16th St.
Philadelphia, PA 19102
(215) 893-5700
Fax: (215) 790-0087

JEWISH JOURNAL
601 Fairway Dr.
Deerfield Beach, FL 33441
(305) 563-3311
Fax: (305) 563-4230

JEWISH NEWS OF
GREATER PHOENIX
1625 E. Northern Ave.
Suite 106
Phoenix, AZ 85020
(602) 870-9470
Fax: (602)870-0426

JEWISH PRESS, THE
333 South 132nd St.
Omaha, NE 68154-2198
(402) 334-8200
Fax: (402) 334-5422

LABOR/COMMUNITY
ALLIANCE
P.O. Box 5077
Fresno, CA 93755
(209) 226-0477
clr@igc.apc.org

Monthly labor/progressive
publication for the Central
San Joaquin Valley.

LA GACETA
P.O. Box 5536
Tampa, FL 33675
(813) 248-3921
Fax: (813) 247-5357
Lagaceta@aol.com

Published in Spanish, English,
and Italian.

LA OPINION
411 West 5th St.
Los Angeles, CA 90013-1000
(213) 622-8332
Fax: (213) 622-2177

Local Spanish daily since 1926.

LA PRENSA
685 S. County Road 427
Longwood, FL 32750
(407) 767-0070
Fax: (407) 767-5478

Local Spanish-language
weekly.

LA PRENSA DE SAN
ANTONIO
113 Lexington Ave.
San Antonio, TX 78207
(210) 242-7900
Fax: (210) 242-7901

Local Spanish-language
weekly.

LA VOZ DE COLORADO
2885 West 3rd Ave.
or P.O. Box 12068
Denver, CO 80219
(303) 936-8556
Fax: (303) 922-9632

Regional bi-lingual weekly.

LA VOZ DE HOUSTON
6101 Southwest Fwy., Suite 127
Houston, TX 77057
(713) 664-4404
Fax: (713) 664-4414

A Spanish-language
publication in Houston.

LA WEEKLY
6715 Sunset Blvd.
Los Angeles, CA 90028
(213) 465-4414
Fax: (213) 465-0044
LAWeekly@aol.com
http://www.laweekly.com

LOUISVILLE ECCENTRIC
OBSERVER
3900 Shelbyville
Louisville, KY 40207
(502) 895-9770
Fax: (502) 895-9779

LEOweekly@aol.com

LONG ISLAND VOICE
393 Jericho Turnpike
Mineola, NY 11501-1205
(516) 877-7373
Fax: (516) 877-0986
http://www.livoice.com

LOS ANGELES SENTINEL
3800 Crenshaw Blvd.
Los Angeles, CA 90008
(213) 299-3800
Fax: (213) 299-3896
Local African-American
weekly.

MEDIAFILE
814 Mission St., Suite 205
San Fransico, CA 94103
(415) 546-6334
Fax: (415) 546-6218
ma@igc.org
http://www.media-alliance.org

Mediafile includes
independent reviews
of Bay Area media issues
including publications,
broadcast outlets, and
internet publishing.

MEMPHIS FLYER
460 Tennessee St.
Memphis, TN 38103
(901) 521-9000
Fax: (901) 521-0129
MemFlyer@aol.com
http://www.memphis
    flyer.com

METRO
550 South First St.
San Jose, CA 95113
(408) 298-8000
Fax: (408) 298-6992
metro@sjmetro.com
http://www.metroactive.com

METROLAND
4 Central Ave., 4th Floor
Albany, NY 12210
(518) 463-2500
Fax: (518) 463-312
metroland@metland.com

METRO PULSE
505 Market St., Suite 300
Knoxville, TN 37902
(423) 522-5399
Fax: (423) 522-2955
info@metropulse.com
http://www.metropulse.com

METRO REPORTER
1366 Turk St.
San Francisco, CA 94115
(415) 931-5778
Fax: (415) 921-0214

Local African-American
weekly.

METRO SANTA CRUZ
111 Union St.
Santa Cruz, CA 95060
(408) 457-9000
Fax: (408) 457-5828

METRO TIMES
733 St. Antione
Detroit, MI 48226
(313) 961-4060
Fax: (313) 964-4849
metrotimes@aminc.com
http://www.metrotimes.com

MIAMI NEW TIMES
2800 Biscayne Blvd., Suite 100
Miami, FL 33137
(305) 576-8000
Fax: (305) 571-7676
editorial@miami-new
    times.com

MIAMI TIMES
900 NW 54th St.
Miami, FL 33127
(305) 757-1147
Fax: (305) 756-0771

Weekly for the African-
American community of
Dade County.

MICHIGAN CHRONICLE
479 Ledyard St.
Detroit, MI 48201-2867
(800) 203-2229
Fax: (313) 963-8788

African-American weekly
since 1936.

MICHIGAN CITIZEN
211 Glendale, Suite 216
Highland Park, MI 48203
(313) 869-0033
Fax: (313) 869-0430

African-American owned
paper.

MISSOULA
INDEPENDENT
115 South 4th West
P.O. Box 8275
Missoula, MT 59801
(406) 543-6609
Fax: (406) 543-4367
info@everyweek.com
http://www.everyweek.com

MONDAY MAGAZINE
1609 Blanshard St.
Victoria, BC V8W2J5 Canada
(250) 382-6188
Fax: (250) 381-2662
sales@monday.com
http://www.monday.com

MONTREAL MIRROR
400 McGill St., #100
Montreal, PQ H2Y 2G1
Canada
(514) 393-1010
Fax: (514) 393-3173
mirror@babylon.montreal.
    qc.ca
http://www.montreal
    mirror.com

MOUNTAIN XPRESS
P.O. Box 144
Asheville, NC 28802
(704) 251-1333
Fax: (704) 251-1311
xpress@circle.net
http://www.circle.net/~xpress

MUNDO HISPANICO
P.O. Box 13808
Atlanta, GA 30324-0808
(404) 881-0441
Fax: (404) 881-6085

Local bilingual weekly.

NASHVILLE SCENE
209 10th Ave. S., Suite 222
Nashville, TN 37203-4101
(615) 244-7989
Fax: (615) 244-8578
Editor@mail.NashScene.com
http://www.nashscene.com

NAVAJO TIMES
Hwy. 264 at Route 12
Window Rock Mall
Window Rock, AZ 86515
(520) 871-6641
Fax: (520) 871-6409

Local American Indian
weekly.

NEW HAVEN ADVOCATE
One Long Wharf Dr.
New Haven, CT 06511
(203) 789-0010
Fax: (203) 787-1418
newhadvo@pcnet.com
http://www.newhaven
   advocate.com

NEW JERSEY JEWISH NEWS
901 Route 10
Whippany, NJ 07881-1157
(201) 887-3900
Fax: (201) 887-5999

NEW PITTSBURGH
COURIER
315 East Carson St.
Pittsburgh, PA 15219
(412) 481-8302
Fax: (412) 481-1360

Bi-weekly African-American
newspaper.

NEW TIMES, BROWARD-
PALM BEACH
16 NE 4th St., Suite 200
Ft. Lauderdale, FL 33301
(954) 233-1600
Fax: (954) 233-1571
http://www.newtimes.com

News, entertainment, investigative journalism.

NEW TIMES,
LOS ANGELES
1950 Sawtelle Blvd., Suite 200
Los Angeles, CA 90025
feedback@newtimesla.com
http://newtimesla.com

NEW TIMES,
SAN LUIS OBISPO
197 Santa Rosa St.
San Luis Obispo, CA 93405
(805) 546-8208
Fax: (805) 546-8641
mail@newtimes-slo.com
http://www.newtimes
   slo.com

NEW TIMES, SYRACUSE
1415 W. Genesee St.
Syracuse, NY 13204-2156
(315) 422-7011
Fax: (315) 422-1721
newtimes@rway.com
http://newtimes.rway.com

NEW YORK BEACON, THE
15 East 40th St., Ste 402
New York, NY 10016
(212) 213-8585
Fax: (212) 213-6291

A weekly tabloid catering to
New York's minority popula-
tion of African-Americans,
Hispanics, and Caribbeans.

NEW YORK PRESS
333 7th Ave., 14th Floor
New York, NY 10001
(212) 244-2282
Fax: (212) 244-9864

NEW YORK VOICE
INC./HARLEM USA
61-17 190th St.
Suite 206
Fresh Meadows, NY 11365
(718) 264-1500
Fax: (718) 264-7708

Covers national and local
news and issues of particular
importance to the African
American community.

NORTH AMERICAN POST
P.O. Box 3173
Seattle, WA 98114
(206) 624-4169
Fax: (206) 625-1424
Asian weekly.

NORTH COAST XPRESS
P.O. Box 1226
Occidental, CA 95465
(707) 874-3104
Fax: (707) 874-1453
doretk@sonic.net

http://www.north-coast
xpress.com/~doretk/

Supports grassroots move-
ments and under-represented
minorities, and exposes
threats to the environment,
an unjust criminal justice
system, and corporate control
of politics and the economy.

NORTHWEST ASIAN
WEEKLY
414 8th Ave. South
Seattle, WA 98104
(206) 223-0623
Fax: (206) 223-0626
Weekly Asian/Pacific Island
newspaper.

NOW
150 Danforth Ave.
Toronto, ON M4K 1N1
Canada
(416) 461-0871
Fax: (416) 461-2886
publisher@now.com
http://www.now.com

NUVO NEWSWEEKLY
811 E. Westfield Blvd.
Indianapolis, IN 46220
(317) 254-2400
Fax: (317) 254-2405
nuvo@nuvo.net
http://www.nuvo-online.com

OAKLAND POST
630 20th St.
Oakland, CA 94612
(510) 287-8200
Fax: (510) 763-9670

OC WEEKLY
151 Kalmus Dr., Suite H10
Costa Mesa, CA 92626
(714) 708-8400
Fax: (714) 708-8410
http://www.ocweekly.com

OJIBWE NEWS, THE
1106 Paul Bunyan Dr., NE
Bemidji, MN 56601
(218) 751-1655
Fax: (218) 251-0650

A weekly native news
publication with focus on
reservation and urban
American Indian communi-
ties within Minnesota.

OKLAHOMA GAZETTE
801 NW 36th St.
Oklahoma City, OK 73118
(405) 528-6000
Fax: (405) 528-4600

OMAHA READER
1618 Harney St.
Omaha, NE 68102
(402) 341-7323
Fax: (402) 341-6967
reader@synergy.net

ORLANDO WEEKLY
807 So. Orlando Ave.
Suite R
Winter Park, FL 32789
(407) 645-5888
Fax: (407) 645-2547
http://www.orlando
    weekly.com

OTHER PAPER, THE
P.O. Box 11376
Eugene, OR 97440
(541) 345-6350
top_staff@efn.org
http://www.efn.org/~topaper

OTTAWA XPRESS
69 Sparks St.
Ottawa, ON K1P 5M5
Canada
(613) 237-8226
Fax: (613) 232-9055
http://www.theottawa
    xpress.ca

PACIFIC NORTHWEST
INLANDER, THE
1003 E. Trent
Suite 110
Spokane, WA 99202
(509) 325-0634
Fax: (509) 325-0638
inlander@iea.com

PACIFIC SUN
21 Corte Madera Ave.
Mill Valley, CA 94941
(415) 383-4500
Fax: (415) 383-4159
PSUN@aol.com
http://www.pacificsun.com

PAPER, THE
325 Commerce Ave. SW
Grand Rapids, MI 49503
(616) 559-0210
Fax: (616) 559-0213
adinfo@the-paper.com
http://www.the-paper.com

PDXS
P.O. Box 10046
Portland, OR 97296
(503) 224-7316
pdxs@teleport.com
http://www.pdxs.com

PHILADELPHIA CITY
PAPER
123 Chestnut St., 3rd Floor
Philadelphia, PA 19106
(215) 735-8444
Fax: (215) 735-8535
adinfo@citypaper.net
http://www.citypaper.net

PHILADELPHIA TRIBUNE,
THE
520 South 16th St.
Philadelphia, PA 19146
(215) 893-4050
Fax: (215) 735-3612

African-American newspaper.

PHILADELPHIA WEEKLY
1701 Walnut St.
Philadelphia, PA 19103
(215) 563-7400
Fax: (215) 563-6799

PHOENIX NEW TIMES
1201 East Jefferson
Phoenix, AZ 85034
(602) 271-0040
Fax: (602) 495-9954
newtimes@newtimes.com
http://www.phoenix
    newtimes.com

PITCHWEEKLY
3535 Broadway, Suite 400
Kansas City, MO 64111
(816) 561-6061
Fax: (816) 756-0502
pitch@pitch.com
http://www.pitch.com

The weekly alternative newspaper for metro Kansas City.

PITTSBURGH CITY PAPER
911 Penn Ave., 6th Floor
Pittsburgh, PA 15222
(412) 560-2489
Fax: (412) 281-1962
info@pghcitypaper.com
http://www.pghcitypaper.com

PORTLAND ALLIANCE,
THE
2807 S. E. Stark St.
Portland, OR 97214
(503) 239-4991
Fax: (503) 232-3764
alliance@teleport.com
http://www.teleport.com/
    ~alliance

Progressive community news.

PORTLAND FREE PRESS
P.O. Box 1327
Tualatin, OR 97062
(503) 625-7692

PRECINCT REPORTER
1677 W. Baseline St.
San Bernadino, CA 92411
(909) 889-0597

African-American/
Caribbean/African.

PROVIDENCE PHOENIX
150 Chestnut St.
Providence, RI 02903
(401) 273-6397
Fax: (401) 351-1399
http://www.providence
    phoenix.com

PUTNAM PIT, THE
P.O. Box 1483
Cookeville, TN 38503
(800) 971-9227
putnampit@reporters.net
http://www.putnampit.com

The watchdog of the Upper
Cumberland, Putnam County.

RANDOM LENGTHS NEWS
1117 South Pacific Ave.
San Pedro, CA 90733
(310) 519-1442
Fax: (310) 832-1000

RENO NEWS & REVIEW
708 North Center St.
Reno, NV 89501
(702) 324-4440
Fax: (702) 324-4572

REUNION
P.O. Box 278
Sudbury, MA 01776
(508) 443-0576
Fax: (508) 443-9857

African-American monthly.

RICHMOND
AFRO-AMERICAN
214 E. Clay St.
Suite 409
Richmond, VA 23219
(804) 649-8478
Fax: (804) 649-8477
Weekly.

RIVERFRONT TIMES
6358 Delmar Blvd.
Suite 200
St. Louis, MO 63130-4719
(314) 615-6666
Fax: (314) 615-6655
http://www.rftstl.com

ROCKY MOUNTAIN
MEDIA WATCH
P.O. Box 18858
Denver, CO 80218
(303) 832-7558
Fax: (303) 832-7558
http://www.imagepage.com/
    rmmw/

RUSSIAN RIVER TIMES
P.O. Box 2130
Guerneville, CA 95446
(707) 869-2010

Bi-monthly.

SACRAMENTO
COMMENT
1114 21st St.
Sacramento, CA 95814
scomment@usa.net
http://www.ns.net/~rrhan

SACRAMENTO
NEWS & REVIEW
1015 20th St.
Sacramento, CA 95814
(916) 498-1234
Fax: (916) 498-7910
NewsReview@aol.com
http://www.newsreview.com

SACRAMENTO OBSERVER
2330 Alhambra Boulevard
Sacramento, CA 95817
(916) 452-4781
Fax: (916) 452-7744

African-American weekly.

SALT LAKE CITY WEEKLY
60 West 400 South
Salt Lake City, UT 84101
(801) 575-7003
Fax: (801) 575-6106
submit@slweekly.com
http://www.slweekly.com

SAN ANTONIO CURRENT
8750 Tesoro Dr., Suite 1
San Antonio, TX 78217
(210) 828-7660
Fax: (210) 828-7883

SAN DIEGO READER
1703 India St.
San Diego, CA 92101
(619) 235-3000
Fax: (619) 231-0489
hrosen@sdreader.com
http://www.sdreader.com

SAN FRANCISCO BAY
GUARDIAN, THE
520 Hampshire
San Francisco, CA 94110
(415) 255-3100
Fax: (415) 255-8762
sfguardian@aol.com
http://www.sfbg.com

SAN FRANCISCO
BAY TIMES
3410 19th St.
San Francisco, CA 94110
(415) 626-0260
Fax: (415) 626-0987
sfbaytimes@aol.co

The Gay/Lesbian/Bi/Trans
newspaper and events calendar for the Bay Area.

SAN FRANCISCO
FRONTLINES
3311 Mission St., Suite 25
San Francisco, CA 94110
(415) 642-3704
Fax: (415) 643-8581
progress@ix.netcom.com
http://www.sf-frontlines.com

A San Francisco Bay Area progressive monthly.

SANTA BARBARA
INDEPENDENT
1221 State St., Suite 200
Santa Barbara, CA 93101
(805) 965-5205
Fax: (805) 965-5518
http://www.independent.com

SANTA FE REPORTER
132 E. Marcy St.
Santa Fe, NM 87501
(505) 988-5541
Fax: (505) 988-5348
71632.223@compuserve.com

SEATTLE SKANNER
1326 Fifth Ave., #825
P.O. Box 12770
Seattle, WA 98101
(206) 233-9888
Fax: (206) 233-9795

African-American weekly.

SEATTLE WEEKLY
1008 Western Ave., Suite 300
Seattle, WA 98104
(206) 623-0500
Fax: (206) 467-4338

SEEN MAGAZINE
331 South Handley
Wichita, KS 67213
(316) 269-4389
Fax: (316) 269-0551
carmody@feist.com
http://www.galaxycorp.com/
    cmkrc

The monthly journal of midwestern infraculture.

SEMINOLE TRIBUNE
6300 Stirling Road
Hollywood, FL 33024
(954) 967-3416
Fax: (954) 967-3482

The newspaper of the
Seminole Tribe of Florida.

SENTRY, THE
74 Montgomery St., #250
San Francisco, CA 94105
(415) 242-0143
Fax: (415) 243-0994
dfp@deathpenalty.org
http://www.deathpenalty.org

Quarterly dedicated to ending
the death penalty.

SEVEN DAYS
P.O. Box 1164
Burlington, VT 05402
(802) 864-5684
Fax: (802) 865-1015
sevenday@together.net
http://www.sevendaysvt.com

SF WEEKLY
185 Berry St., Suite 3800
San Francisco, CA 94107
(415) 541-0700
Fax: (415) 777-1839

SHEPHERD EXPRESS
1123 North Water St.
Milwaukee, WI 53202
(414) 276-2222
Fax: (414) 276-3312
doug@shepherd-express.com
http://www.shepherd
    express.com

SHO-BAN NEWS
P.O. Box 900
Fort Hall, ID 83203
(208) 238-3701
Fax: (208) 238-3702

Shoshone-Bannock Tribes—
weekly.

SHUNPIKING DISCOVERY
MAGAZINE
P.O. Box 31377
Halifax, NS B3K 5Z1
Canada
(902) 455-4922
Fax: (902) 455-7599

Discusses social issues
surrounding the natural
resources and society
of Nova Scotia.

SLINGSHOT NEWSPAPER
3124 Shattuck Ave.
Berkeley, CA 94705
(510) 540-0751
resist@burn.ucsd.edu

SONOMA COUNTY
INDEPENDENT, THE
540 Mendocino Ave.
Santa Rosa, CA 95401
(707) 527-1200
Fax: (707) 527-1288
indy@livewire.com
http://www.metroactive.com/
    sonoma

A forum for environmental
issues with both regional and
national scope—published 11
times a year.

SONOMA VALLEY VOICE
P.O. Box 907
Boyes Host Springs, CA 95416
(707) 996-9678
Fax: (707) 996-8859

Alternative news and opinion
quarterly.

STRANGER, THE
1202 East Pike
Suite 1225
Seatlle, WA 98122
(206) 323-7101
Fax: (206) 325-4865
http://www.thestranger.com

ST. SPIRIT
65 Ninth St.
San Francisco, CA 94103
(415) 565-0201
Fax: (415) 565-0204
spirit@afsc-pmr.org

Justice news and homeless
blues in the San Francisco
Bay Area.

SUN REPORTER, THE
1791 Bancroft Ave.
San Francisco, CA 94124
(415) 671-1000
Fax: (415) 931-0214

The original African-
American weekly in S.F.

SURVIVAL NEWS
95 Standard St.
Mattapan, MA 02126
(617) 289-7311
masswelf@aol.com

Welfare rights news and
grass roots organizing.

TENNESSEE
TRIBUNE, THE
1818 Morena St.
A.J. Cebrun
Journalism Center
Nashville, TN 37208

(615) 321-3268
Fax: (615) 321-0409
African-American weekly.

TEXAS OBSERVER
307 W. Seventh St.
Austin, TX 78701
(512) 477-0746
Fax: (512) 474-1175
observer@eden.com
http://www.hyperweb.com/
    txobserver

TIMES OF ACADIANA
P.O. Drawer 3528
Lafayette, LA 70502
(318) 237-3560
Fax: (318) 261-2630
toaedit@aol.com

TRANSPORTATION
ALTERNATIVES
115 West 30th St., #1207
New York, NY 10001
(212) 629-3311
Fax: (212) 629-8334
info@transalt.org
http://www.transalt.org

News and advocacy for
greater use of human-powered
transportation in New York
City.

TREASURE STATE
REVIEW
P.O. Box 99
Big Fork, MT 59911

A Montana periodical
devoted to journalism
and justice.

TRI-STATE DEFENDER
124 East Calhoun Ave
Memphis, TN 38103
(901) 523-1818
Fax: (901) 523-1520

African-American weekly.

TRI-VALLEY CARE'S
CITIZEN'S WATCH
5720 East Ave., #116
Livermore, CA 94550
(510) 443-0177
Fax: (510) 443-0177
marylia@igc.org

TUCSON WEEKLY
P.O. Box 2429
Tucson, AZ 85702
(520) 792-3630
Fax: (520) 792-2096
sales@tucsonweekly.com
http://www.tucson
    weekly.com

TUNDRA TIMES
P.O. Box 92247
Anchorage, AK 99509-2247
(907) 349-2512
Fax: (907) 349-0335

Bi-weekly—the leading voice
for Alaska Native rights and
social progress.

VALLEY ADVOCATE
87 School St.
Hatfield, MA 01038
(413) 247-9301
Fax: (413) 247-5439
http://valleyadvocate.com

V. MAGAZINE
P.O. Box 14393
Irvine, CA 92643
(714) 541-9210
Fax: (714) 839-1917

Bi-monthly.

VOICE OF THE WILD
SISKIYOU
P.O. Box 220
Cave Junction, OR 97523
(541) 592-4459
Fax: (541) 592-2653
project@siskiyou.org
http://www.siskiyou.org

Quarterly newsletter of the
Siskiyou Regional Education
Project.

VOIR MONTRÉAL
4130 Saint-Denis
Montreal, PQ H2W 2M5
Canada
(514) 848-0805
Fax: (514) 848-9004
http://www.voir.ca

VOIR QUEBEC
35 Cote du Palais
Quebec, PQ G1R 4H9
Canada
(418) 694-0557
Fax: (418) 694-0634
http://www.voir.ca

WASHINGTON AFRO-
AMERICAN
1612 14th St., NW, 2nd floor
Washington, DC 20009
(202) 332-0080
Fax: (202) 939-7461

WASHINGTON
CITY PAPER
2390 Champlain St., NW
Washington, DC 20009
(202) 332-2100
Fax: (202) 462-8323
mail@washcp.com
http://www.washington
    citypaper.com

WASHINGTON
FREE PRESS
1463 East Republican, #178
Seattle, WA 98112
(206) 860-5290
freepres@scn.org
http://www.speakeasy.org/
    wfp

Reports the underreported
events of the Northwest
specializing in labor and
environmental topics.

WASHINGTON
INFORMER
3117 M.L. King Ave., SE
Washington, DC 20032
(202) 561-4100
Fax: (202) 574-3785

African-American weekly.

WAUSAU CITY PAGES
300 3rd St., lower level
P.O. Box 942
Wausau, WI 54402-0942
(715) 845-5171
Fax: (715) 848-5887
citypages@pcpros.net

WEEK, THE
8811 Colesville Rd.
Suite 115
P.O. Box 7183
Silver Spring, MD 20910
(301) 565-2753
Fax: (301) 589-4278

African-American weekly.

WEEKLY ALIBI
2118 Central Ave. SE
Suite 151
Albuquerque, NM 87106
(505) 268-8111
Fax: (505) 256-9651
http://desert.net/alibi

WEEKLY PLANET
1310 E. 9th Ave.
Tampa, FL 33605
(813) 248-8888
Fax: (813) 248-9999

WEST SIDE EYE
210 West 83rd St.
Lower Level
New York, NY 10024
(212) 769-2044
Fax: (212) 712-0593
aaron@humanism.org
http://humanism.org/
    WestSideEye

A free all-volunteer
humanist newspaper
for the West Side.

WESTWORD
1621 18th St., Suite 150
Denver, CO 80202
(303) 296-7744
Fax: (303) 296-5416
http://www.westword.com

WE THE PEOPLE
P.O. Box 8218
Santa Rosa, CA 95407
(707) 573-8896
wtppub@aol.com

WILLAMETTE WEEK
822 SW 10th Ave.
Portland, OR 97205
(503) 243-2122
Fax: (503) 243-1115

WIND RIVER NEWS
453 Main St.
Lander, WY 82520
(307) 332-2323
Fax: (307) 332-2323

A weekly newspaper that
serves the members of the
Shoshone and Arapaho Tribes.

WOMEN'S VOICES,
SONOMA COUNTY
P.O. Box 4448
Santa Rosa, CA 95402-4448
(707) 575-5654
wv@monitor.net

WORCESTER MAGAZINE
172 Shrewsbury St.
Worcester, MA 01604
(508) 755-8004
Fax: (508) 755-8860

RCESTER PHOENIX
14 Washington St.
Auburn, MA 01501
(508) 832-9800
Fax: (508) 832-5510
http://www.worcester
     phoenix.com

YO!: YOUTH OUTLOOK
660 Market St., Suite 210
San Francisco, CA 94104
(415) 243-4364
Fax: (415) 243-0815
yo@pacificnews.org
http://www.pacific.news/yo/

A publication by and about
California's young people.

YOLK
P.O. Box 861555
Los Angeles, CA 90086
(310) 917-7252
Fax: (213) 223-7900

Asian quarterly.

YSB
1 BET Plaza
1900 W. Pl., NE
Washington, DC
20018-1211
(202) 608-2000
Fax: (202) 608-2598

African-American monthly.

ORGANIZATIONS AND ACTIVIST GROUPS

50 YEARS IS ENOUGH:
U.S. Network For Global
Economic Justice
1025 Vermont Ave., NW
Suite 300
Washington, DC 20005
(202) 879-3187
Fax: (202) 879-3186
wb50years@igc.apc.org

A network of 200 social
and economic justice
organizations.

ACCION ZAPATISTA
312 E. 43rd St., #203
Austin, TX 78751
(512) 303-9547
ave@uts.cc.utexas.edu/
     student/nave/
http://www.utexas.edu/ftp/n

Zapatista solidarity
information, communiques,
history, and links with
liberation struggles.

ADVOCATES FOR YOUTH
1025 Vermont Ave., NW
Suite 200
Washington, DC 20005
(202) 347-5700
Fax: (202) 347-2263
info@advocatesforyouth.org
http://www.advocates
     foryouth.org

Seeks to support and
educate teens and
adolescents regarding
sexuality, reproduction,
and sexually transmitted
diseases.

AFRICA NEWS SERVICE
P.O. Box 3851
Durham, NC 27702
(919) 286-0747
Fax: (919) 286-2614
newsdesk@afnews.org
http://www.africanews.org

Disseminates stories from
African news organizations.

ACCURACY IN MEDIA
4455 Connecticut Ave., NW
Suite 330
Washington, DC 20005
(202) 364-4401
Fax: (202) 364-4098
ar@aim.org
http://www.aim.org

Provides media analysis and
investigation from a right-
wing perspective

A-INFOS RADIO PROJECT
http://www.radio4all.org/

This alternative to satellite
downlinking provides micro-
broadcasters with a means to
distribute and archive broadcast quality radio programming via the Internet.

ALLIANCE FOR
DEMOCRACY
731 State St.
Madison,WI 53703
(608) 262-9036
Fax: (608) 251-3267
alliance-democracy@
     wigate.nic.wisc.edu

http://www.sit.wisc.edu/
    ~democrac/

A student sponsored
organization dedicated to
stopping the corporatization
of colleges and universities.

ALTERNATIVE RADIO
David Barsamian
2129 Mapleton
Boulder, CO 80304
(303) 444-8788

Cassettes and transcripts of
programs with movement
activists and scholars like
Noam Chomsky, Helen
Caldicott, Ralph Nader,
Angela Davis, Howard Zinn,
Winona LaDuke, Manning
Marable and many others.
Free catalog.

ALTERNATIVE
MEDIA, INC.
P.O. Box 21308
Washington, DC 20009
(202) 588-9807
Fax: (202) 588-9809
mpaulsen@aminc.com

ALTERNATIVE PRESS
CENTER
P.O. Box 33109
1443 Gorsuch Ave
Baltimore, MD 21218
(410) 243-2471
Fax: (410) 235-5325
altpress@altpress.org
http://www.altpress.org/

Publishes the quarterly
Alternative Press Index,
a database which covers 270
periodicals with central focus
on socialism, liberation
struggles, labor, indigenous
peoples, gays/lesbians,
feminism, ecology, anti-
racism, and anarchism.
Co-publishes with the
Independent Press Association
*Annotations, A Guide to the
Independent Critical Press.*

ALTERNATIVES IN PRINT
TASK FORCE OF THE
AMERICAN LIBRARY
ASSOCIATION'S SOCIAL
RESPONSIBILITIES ROUND
TABLE
1716 SW Williston Road
Gainesville, FL 32608-4049
(352) 335-2200
http://www.LibLib.com

Advocates local selection and
cataloging of materials from
small and alternative presses
and independent producers
by sponsoring programs and
Internet discussions; liking
grassroots groups; and
producing reviews, articles,
exhibits, on-line resources,
the biennial directory
Alternative Publishers of
Books in North America
(CRISES Press), etc. Publishes
quarterly review journal,
Counterpoise.

ALTERNET
Keri Hayes, Managing Editor
77 Federal St.
San Francisco, CA 94107
(415) 284-1420
Fax: (415) 284-1414
khayes@igc.org
http://www.igc.org/an/

An online news and
syndication service for the
independent press. A project
of the Independent Media
Institute, AlterNet offers
about 30 new stories a week.

AMERICAN FRIENDS
SERVICE COMMITTEE
(AFSC)
1501 Cherry St.
Philadelphia, PA 19102
(215) 241-7000
Fax: (215) 241-7275
afscinfo@afsc.org
http://www.afsc.org

A national Quaker organization that includes people of
various faiths who are dedicated to humanitarian service
and social justice issues.

AMERICAN HELLENIC
MEDIA PROJECT
P.O. Box 1150
New York, NY 10028
ahmp@hri.org
http://www.hri.org/ahmp/

A grassroots, not-for-profit
think tank created to educate
the media regarding
American-Hellenic issues.

AMERICAN LIBRARY
ASSOCIATION OFFICE
FOR INTELLECTUAL
FREEDOM
50 East Huron St.
Chicago, IL 60611
(312) 280-4223
(800) 545-2433
Fax: (312) 280-4227
oif@ala.org
http://www.ala.org/oif.html

Organized to educate
librarians and the general
public about the nature and
importance of intellectual
freedom in libraries.

AMERICAN LIBRARY
ASSOCIATION
(Washington Office)
Office for Information
Technology Policy
Carol Henderson, Director
1301 Pennsylvania Ave., NW
Suite 403
Washington, DC 20004-1701
(202) 628-8410
Fax: (202) 628-8419
http://www.ala.org/washoff/

AMERICAN SOCIETY
OF JOURNALISTS
AND AUTHORS
1501 Broadway
Suite 302
New York, NY 10036
(212) 997-0947
Fax: (212) 768-7414
102535.2427@compuserve.com
http://www.asja.org

Produces a membership
directory, including a list of
1000 non-fiction freelance
writers, with their phone, fax,
and writing specialty.

AMNESTY
INTERNATIONAL
304 Pennsylvania Ave., SE
Washington, DC 20003
(800) 266-3789
(202) 544-0200
Fax: (202) 546-7142
admin-us@aiusa.org
Memberships:
aimember@aiusa.org
http://www.amnesty.org

An international organization
which works to ensure
human rights throughout the
world and opposes human
rights abuses.

APPLIED RESEARCH
CENTER
1322 Webster St.
Suite 402
Oakland, CA 94612
(510) 465-9577
Fax: (510) 465-4824
arc@arc.org
http://www.arc.org

A public policy, education,
and reseach institute which
emphasizes issues of race and
social change.

ARIZONA MEDIA ACTION
David Winkler
P.O. Box 80496
Phoenix, AZ 85060-0496
(602) 996-5823
mediamaven@home.com

ASIAN AMERICAN
JOURNALISTS
ASSOCIATION
1765 Sutter St., Suite 1000
San Francisco, CA 94115
(415) 346-2051
Fax: (415) 931-4671
aaja1@aol.com
http://www.aaja.org/

Committed to insuring diversity in american journalism and expressing the Asian-American perspective.

ASSOCIATION FOR
EDUCATION JOURNALISM
AND MASS
COMMUNICATION
1621 College St.
Columbia, SC 29208
(803) 777-2005

Deals mainly with research topics in mass communications.

ASSOCIATION OF
ALTERNATIVE
NEWSWEEKLIES
1660 L St., NW, Suite 316
Washington, DC 20036
(202) 822-1955
Fax: (202) 822-0929
ann@intr.net
http://aan.org

A coordinating and administrative organization for 113 alternative newsweeklies in the U.S. and Canada.

ASSOCIATION OF
AMERICAN PUBLISHERS
71 Fifth Ave.
New York, NY 10003
(212) 255-0200
Fax: (212) 255-7007
jplatt@publishers.org
http://www.publishers.org/

A national trade association dedicated to protection of intellectual property rights and defense of free expression.

BALANCE & ACCURACY
IN JOURNALISM
P.O. Box 824
Carrboro, NC 27510
(919) 968-4062
mediashun@mindspring.com

BENTON FOUNDATION
1634 Eye St., NW, 11th Fl.
Washington, DC 20006
(202) 638-5770
Fax: (202) 638-5771
benton@benton.org
http://www.benton.org

A private foundation that works to shape the emerging communications environments to realize the social benefits made possible by the public interest use of communications.

BERKELEY MEDIA
STUDIES GROUP
2140 Shattuck Ave.
Suite 804
Berkeley, CA 94704
(510) 204-9700
Fax: (510) 204-9710
bmsg@bmsg.org

Focuses on public health and
social issues.

BEYONDMEDIA
59 East Van Buren, #1400
Chicago, IL 60605
(312) 922-7780

A video production
organization focused on
public awareness of women's
and girl's social change
initiatives.

BLACK WOMEN IN
PUBLISHING
P.O. Box 6275, FDR Station
New York, NY 10150
(212) 772-5951
bwip@hotmail.com
http://www.bwip.org

An employee-based trade
association dedicated to
increasing the presence—
and supporting the efforts—
of African heritage women
and men in the publishing
industry.

CALIFORNIA FIRST
AMENDMENT
COALITION
2701 Cottage Way
Suite 12
Sacramento, CA 95825-1226
(916) 974-8888
Fax: (916) 974-880
wzlotlow@cfac.org or
tfrancke@cfac.org
http://www.cfac.org

California jouralist's legal
notebook and annual conference to California's First
Amendment Conference.

CAMPUS ALTERNATIVE
JOURNALISM PROJECT
P.O. Box 425748
Cambridge, MA 02142
(617) 725-2886
Fax: (617) 547-5067
cco@igc.apc.org
http://www.cco.org

Supports the work of campus
progressive activists who
make their own printed
media.

CENTER FOR
COMMERCIAL-FREE
PUBLIC EDUCATION
360 Grand Ave.
P.O. Box 385
Oakland, CA 94610
(510) 268-1100
Fax: (510) 268-1277
unplug@igc.apc.org

Provides support to students, parents, teachers and others concerned, organizing across the U.S. to keep their schools commercial-free and community controlled.

CENTER FOR
CONSTITUTIONAL
RIGHTS
666 Broadway, 7th floor
New York, NY 10012
(212) 614-6464
ccr@igc.apc.org

A non-profit legal and educational organization dedicated to advancing and protecting the rights guaranteed by the United States Constitution and the Universal Declaration of Human Rights, and to the creative use of law as a postive force for social change.

CENTER FOR DEFENSE
INFORMATION
1500 Massachusetts Ave., NW
Washington, DC 20005
(202) 862-0700
(800) CDI-3334
Fax: (202) 862-0708
info@cdi.org
http://www.cdi.org

Opposes excessive military expenditures that increase the dangers of war.

CENTER FOR
DEMOCRATIC VALUES
5700 Cass Ave., Room 2426
Detroit, MI 48202
(313) 577-0828
Fax: (313) 577-8585
RAronso@cll.wayne.edu
http://www.igc.apc.org/cdv

CENTER FOR
INTEGRATION AND
IMPROVEMENT OF
JOURNALISM
Journalism Department
San Francisco State Univ.
1600 Holloway Ave.
San Francisco, CA 94132
(415) 338-2083
Fax: (415) 338-2084
iroman@sfsu.edu
http://www.journalism.
    sfsu.edu
http://www.newswatch.
    sfsu.edu

A series of model programs designed to bring ethnic diversity to the country's newsrooms and promote a fair and balanced coverage of our multicultural society.

CENTER FOR
INTERNATIONAL POLICY
1755 Massachusetts Ave., NW
Washington, DC 20036
(202) 232-3312
Fax: (202) 232-3440
cip@igc.apc.org
http://www.us.net/cip

Promotes a U.S. foreign policy that reflects democratic values.

CENTER FOR INVESTIGATIVE REPORTING
500 Howard St.
Suite 206
San Francisco, CA 94105
(415) 543-1200
Fax: (415) 543-8311
CIR@igc.org
http://www.muckraker.org/
    pubs/papertrails/
    index.html

Exposes abuse of power in bureaucracy by working with local and national media focusing on public accountability.

CENTER FOR MEDIA AND THE BLACK EXPERIENCE
4357 Luxemburg Dr.
Decatur, GA 30034
(404) 526-5470

CENTER FOR MEDIA AND DEMOCRACY
3318 Gregory St.
Madison, WI 53711
(608) 233-3346
Fax: (608) 238-2236
stauber@compuserve.com
http://www.prwatch.org

Specializes in "blowing the lid off today's multi-billion dollar propoganda-for-hire industry."

CENTER FOR MEDIA AND PUBLIC AFFAIRS
2100 L St., NW, Suite 300
Washington, DC MD 20037
(202) 223-2942
Fax: (202) 872-4014
cmpamm@aol.com
http://www.cmpa.com/
    html/2100.html

Bridges the gap between academic research and the broader domains of media and public policy.

CENTER FOR MEDIA CULTURE AND HISTORY
25 Waverly Pl., #501
New York, NY 10003
(212) 998-3759
ba2@is.nyu.edu
http://www.nyu.edu/gsas/
    program/media/

Focuses on the role that media play in shaping our perceptions of history and culture; in forging individual, collective, national, and transnational identities; and in mediating the direction and character of social change.

CENTER FOR MEDIA EDUCATION
1511 K St. NW, Suite 518
Washington, DC 20005
(202) 628-2620
Fax: (202) 628-2554
cme@cme.org
http://www.cme.org/cme

Publishes "InfoActive Kids" a quarterly print publication for the child advocacy, consumer, health and educational communities.

CENTER FOR MEDIA LITERACY
4727 Wilshire Blvd.
Suite #403
Los Angeles, CA 90010
(213) 931-4177
Fax: (213) 931-4474
cml@medialit.org
http://www.medialit.org

Encouraging critical thinking in academic environments with videos and books that focus on democratic processes.

CENTER FOR PUBLIC INTEGRITY
1634 I St. NW, Suite 902
Washington, DC 20006
(202) 783-3900
Fax: (202) 783-3906
contact@publicintegrity.org
http://www.public
    integrity.org

Coverage of important national issues by responsible journalists published in full form without the traditional time and space limitations.

CENTER FOR RESPONSIVE POLITICS
1320 19th St., NW, Suite 700
Washington, DC 20036

(202) 857-0044
Fax: (202) 857-7809
http://www.crp.org

Nonpartisan, nonprofit research group that specializes in the study of Congress and the role that money plays in its elections and actions.

CENTER FOR SCIENCE IN THE PUBLIC INTEREST
1875 Connecticut Ave. NW
Suite 300
Washington, DC 20009
(202) 332-9110
Fax: (202) 265-4954
cspi@cspinet.org
http://www.cspinet.org

Dedicated to supporting science and scientists who actively participate in promoting the public interest and general welfare.

CENTER FOR THE PRESERVATION OF MODERN HISTORY
P.O. Box 23511
Santa Barbara, CA 93121
(805) 899-3433
Fax: (805) 899-4773
patrick@silcom.com
http://www.prevailing
    winds.org

Produces research and exposés on U.S. government corruption and malfeasance

CENTER FOR THIRD
WORLD ORGANIZING
1218 East 21st St.
Oakland, CA 94606-9950
(510) 533-7583
Fax: (510) 533-0923
ctwo@igc.org
http://www.igc.org/ctwo

Innovative organizer training
and leadership programs in
communities of color.

CENTER FOR WAR, PEACE
AND THE NEWS MEDIA
10 Washington Place, 4th Fl.
New York, NY 10003
(212) 998-7960
Fax: (212) 995-4143
war.peace.news@nyu.edu
http://www.nyu.edu/
    globalbeat

Dedicated to supporting journalists and news organizations
in their efforts to sustain an
informed citizenry.

CENTER OF CONCERN
(COC)
700 13th St., NE
Washington, DC 20017
(202) 635-2757
Fax: (202) 832-9494
coc@igc.apc.org
http://www.igc.org/coc/
Social analysis, theological
reflection, policy advocacy,
and public education on
issues of development, peace
and justice.

CHIAPAS MEDIA PROJECT
4834 N. Springfield
Chicago, IL 60625
(773) 583-7728
Fax: 773-583-7738
alex2051@xsite.net
http://www.chiapasmedia
    project.org/

A bi-national partnership
that provides tools and
training so that marginalized
indigenous communities can
establish their own
information outlets. The
project provides video
cameras, editing equipment,
computers and appropriate
training so that communities
in Chiapas can tell their own
stories in their own words.

CHICAGO MEDIA WATCH
P.O. Box 268737
Chicago, IL 60626
(773) 604-1910
cmw@mediawatch.org
http://www.mediawatch.org/
    chicago

Chicago-based media activist
group which publishes a quarterly newsletter on grassroots
media activism and vital public infromation that the mainstream press chooses to omit,
distort or ignore.

CITIZEN VAGROM
1111 East Madison
Seattle, WA 98122
(206) 344-6434

citizen@speakeasy.org
http://eve.speakeasy.org/
citizen/vagrom/index.html

A grassroots response to corporate-dominated media. Vagrom's purpose is to generate public debate on media and democracy, and to build alternatives to profit-dr.n communications.

CITIZENS' COUNCIL ON CORPORATE ISSUES
2651 W. 5th Ave.
Vancouver, BC V6K 1T2,
Canada
gil_yaron@bc.sympatico.ca

Dedicated to reopening the debate around the consequences of the corporate form. Our mandate is to conduct research on and educate the general public about the impacts of the corporation on society, including the role of corporate media.

CITIZENS FOR INDEPENDENT PUBLIC BROADCASTING
c/o Center for Social Studies Education
901 Old Hickory Road
Pittsburgh, PA 15243
(412) 341-1967
jmstarr@aol.com

Coordinates a national campaign to educate policy makers and members of the public to the need to restructure public broadcasting as a federal trust, subsidized by the profits of the commercial broadcasting industry.

CITIZENS FOR MEDIA LITERACY
34 Wall St., Suite 407
Asheville, NC 28801
(704) 255-0182
Fax: (704) 254-2286
cml@main.nc.us
http://www.main.nc.us/cml

CITIZENS' MEDIA CORPS
c/o Steve Provizer
23 Winslow Rd.
Brookline, MA 02446
(617) 232-3174
http://www.radfrall.org/

Seeks out the most politically and culturally disenfranchised citizens and community groups and provides them with the tools necessary to both access mainstream media and to create alternative media outlets.

THE CIVIC MEDIA CENTER & LIBRARY, INC.
1021 W. University Ave.
Gainesville, FL 32601
(352) 373-0010
cmc@afn.org
http://www.afn.org/~cmc

A non-profit library and reading room of alternative press publications. Contains books, periodicals, reference materials (including the Alternative Press Index), 'zine library, and an audio & video collection.

COMMITTEE TO PROTECT JOURNALISTS
330 Seventh Ave., 12th Floor
New York, NY 10001
(212) 465-1004
Fax: (212) 465-9568
info@cpj.org
http://www.cpj.org

Monitors violations of press freedom and of journalists' human rights both nationally and internationally.

COMMON CAUSE
1250 Connecticut Ave, NW
6th Floor
Washington, DC 20036
(202) 833-1200
Fax: (202) 659-3716
http://www.commoncause.org

Supports open, accountable government and the right of all American citizens to be involved in helping to shape the nation's public policies.

COMMUNICATIONS CONSORTIUM AND MEDIA CENTER
1333 H St., MW, Suite 700
Washington, DC 20005
Fax: (202) 682-1270
http://www.womenofcolor.
   org/about.html

COMMUNITY MEDIA WORKSHOP AT COLUMBIA COLLEGE
600 South Michigan Ave.
Chicago, IL 60605-1996
(312) 344-6400
Fax: (312) 344-6404
cmw@newstips.org
http://www.newstips.org

Trains community organizations and civic groups to use media more effectively and helps journalists learn of their stories. Publishers of *Getting On The Air & Into Print*, a 200-page citizen's guide to Chicago-area media.

CONEXION LATINA/
LATIN AMERICA CONNEXIONS
2344 Spruce St.
Vancouver, BC V6H 2P2, Canada
(604) 682-3269
Fax: (604) 733-1852
conexion@vcn.bc.ca

An alternative media project produced by a volunteer collective including Latin Americans and Canadians. We support movements which resist the current global system of economic injustice and social, political and cultural oppression.

CONSEIL DE PRESSE DE
QUEBEC
C239 Montreal
Quebec, PQ H2K 3L7 Canada
(514) 529-2818
Fax: (514) 873-4434
info@conseildepresse.qc.ca
http://www.conseil
   depresse.qc.ca

CONSUMER PROJECT ON
TECHNOLOGY
P.O. Box 19367
Washington, DC 20036
(202) 387-8030
Fax: (202) 234-5176
love@cptech.org
http://www.cptech.org

Focuses on intellectual property, telecommunications,
privacy and electronic commerce.

CONSUMER'S UNION
OF UNITED STATES, INC.
101 Truman Ave.
Yonkers, NY 10703
(914) 378-2000
Fax: (914) 378-2900
http://www.consunion.org

Advances the interests
of consumers by providing
information and advice about
products and services and
about issues affecting their
welfare.

COUNCIL ON
INTERNATIONAL AND
PUBLIC AFFAIRS
P.O. Box 246
S. Yarmouth, MA 02664
(508) 398-1145
Fax: (508) 398-1552
people@poclad.org

Instigating democratic
conversations and actions
that contest the authority
of corporations to govern.

CULTURAL
ENVIRONMENT
MOVEMENT
3508 Market St., Suite 3-030
Phildelphia, PA 19104
(215) 204-6434
Fax: (215) 387-1560
ggerbner@nimbus.Temple.edu

A broad-based international
coalition of citizens, scholars,
activists, and media
professionals who promote
democratic principles in the
cultural environment.

DEMOCRACY NOW
Hosted by Amy Goodman
http://www.webactive.com/pa
cifica/demnow.html

Launched by Pacifica Radio in
1996 to open the airwaves on a
daily basis to alternative voices
traditionally excluded from the
political process, programs
with Amy Goodman are now
available online.

DIRECT ACTION MEDIA
NETWORK (DAMN!)
http://damn.tao.ca/

An on-line multi-media news
service that covers direct
actions that progressive
organizations and individuals
take to attain a peaceful, open
and enlightened society.

DOWNTOWN
COMMUNITY TV CENTER
87 Lafayette St.
New York, NY 10013
(212) 966-4510
http://www.dctvny.org

Founded in 1972, DCTV
believes that expanding public
access to the electronic media
arts invigorates our democracy. DCTV pursues a grass-
roots mission to teach people,
particularly members of low-
income and minority communities, how to use media.

DURLAND ALTERNATIVES
LIBRARY
A Community Resource,
Free and Open to All
127 Anabel Taylor Hall
Cornell University Campus
Ithaca, NY 14853
(607) 255-6486
Fax: (607) 255-9985
alt-lib@cornell.edu
http://instruct1.cit.cornell.
edu/courses/altlib

Dedicated to providing hard-
to-find books and other materials that deal with contemporary issues and topics con-
cerning alternative lifestyles,
health, education, community, minority and other under-
represented groups, politics;
peace, gender, spirituality,
etc. The original collection
was built around the manifes-
tations of counter-culture
trends and thought of the late
1960s and early 1970s.

EARTH FIRST!
P.O. Box 1415
Eugene, OR 97401
(541) 344-8004
Fax: (541) 344-7688
earthfirst@igc.apc.org
http://www.enviroweb.org/ef/

The voice of the radical environmental movement.

ECHO MOUNTAIN
PRODUCTIONS, INC.
1223 Wilshire Blvd., #924
Santa Monica, CA 90403
(310) 453-4272
echoprod@compuserve.com
http://www.ballona.com

Produces documentaries, public service announcements,
and children's programming
related to the environment
and sustainability. Latest
film is *The Last Stand—
The Struggle for Ballona
Wetlands*, hosted by Edward
Asner.

ECONOMIC POLICY
INSTITUTE
1660 L St., NW
Washington, DC 20036
(202) 331-5549
Fax: (202) 775-0819
http://www.epinet.org

Its mission is to broaden public debate over economic policy to better serve the needs of America's working people. It also seeks to expose the myths behind the supposed success of the neoliberal economic paradigm.

ELECTRONIC FRONTIER
FOUNDATION
1550 Bryant St., Suite 725
San Francisco, CA 94103
(415) 436-9333
Fax: (415) 436-9993
eff@eff.org
http://www.eff.org

A leading civil liberties organization devoted to maintaining the internet as a global vehicle for free speech.

FAIRNESS AND
ACCURACY IN
REPORTING (FAIR)
130 West 25th St.
New York, NY 10001
(212) 633-6700
Fax: (212) 727-7668
fair@fair.org
http://www.fair.org

A national media watchdog group that focuses public awareness on "the narrow corporate ownership of the press..." FAIR seeks to invigorate the First Amendment by advocating for greater media pluralism and the inclusion of public interest voices in national debate. FAIR's Local Activist Contacts:

Chicago: Liane Casten
(312) 604-1910

Dallas: B.J. Armstrong
(817) 295-1602

D.C.: Sarah Durand
(202) 544-0796

Corvallis, OR: Tom Blazier
(541) 752-3152
tblazier@peak.org

Ithaca, N.Y.: Will Burbank
(607) 272-7555
Bluebird@lightlink.com

L.A.: Jim Horwitz
(310) 445-9109
succeednow@aol.com

Minneapolis: Mary Shepard
(612) 454-3918

New York: New York Free
Media Alliance
(212) 969-8636

Pittsburgh: Jerry Starr
(412) 341-1967
jmstarr@aol.com

FEDERAL
COMMUNICATIONS
COMMISSION
Visit the Man.
http://www.fcc.gov/

FEMINISTS FOR FREE
EXPRESSION
2525 Times Square Station
New York, NY 10108
(212) 702-6292
Fax: (212) 702-6277
FFE@aol.com
http://www.well.com/user/l
    freedom

A national organization of
feminist women and men
who share a commitment
both to gender equality and
to preserving the individual's
right and to read, view, rent,
or purchase media materials
of their choice, free from
government intervention.

FLYING FOCUS VIDEO
COLLECTIVE
3439 NE Sandy Blvd., #248
Portland, OR 97232
(503) 321-5051
Fax: (503) 239-7456
ffvc@agora.rdrop.com
http://www.rdrop.com/
    ~ffvc
Uses video as a tool for
social change.

FREE SPEECH TV
P.O. Box 6060
Boulder, CO 80306
(303) 442-8445
Fax: (303) 442-6472
programming@fstv.org
http://www.freespeech.org

Progressive voice in the
media revolution bringing
activist & alternative media
into seven million homes
each week.

FREEDOM FORUM WORLD
CENTER
1101 Wilson Blvd.
Arlington, VA 22209
(703) 528-0800
Fax: (703) 522-4831
news@freedomforumu.org
http://www.freedomforum.org

A nonpartisan, international
foundation dedicated to free
press, free speech and free
spirit for all people.

FREEDOM OF EXPRESSION
FOUNDATION
171-B Claremont Ave.
Long Beach, CA 90803
(562) 434-2284
crsmith@csulb.edu
http://www.csulb.edu/
    ~research/Cent/
    lamend.html

Publishes a number of studies
on freedom of expression in
America and a newsletter that
deals with issues of the day.

FREEDOM OF
INFORMATION CENTER
at University of Missouri
127 Neff Annex
Columbia, MO 65211
(573) 882-4856
Fax: (573) 884-4963
Kathleen_Edwards@jmail.
    jour.missouri.edu
http://www.missouri.edu/
    ~foiwww

Collects and indexes materials relating to controls on the flow and content of information to research free-press issues.

FREEDOM OF
INFORMATION
CLEARINGHOUSE
P.O. Box 19367
Washington, DC 20036
(202) 588-7790
foia@citizen.org
http://www.citizen.org/
    public_citizen/litigation/
    foic/foic.html

FREEDOM TO READ
FOUNDATION
Judith Krug, Executive
Director and Secretary
50 East Huron St.
Chicago, IL 60611
(312) 944-6780
Fax: (312) 280-4392
webmaster@ala.org
http://www.ala.org/alaorg/
    oif/ftrf_home.html

Promotes and protects freedom of speech and freedom of the press; protects the public's right of access to libraries; supplies legal counsel and otherwise supports libraries and librarians suffering injustices due to their defense of freedom of speech and of the press (run by ALA, but a separate organization—does 1st Amendment litigation).

FUND FOR INVESTIGATIVE
JOURNALISM
5120 Kenwood Dr.
Annandale, VA 22003
(703) 750-3849
fundfij@aol.com
http://www.fij.org

Gives grants to journalists seeking help for investigative pieces involving environmental issues, corruption, malfeasance, incompetence and societal ills in general as well as for media criticism.

GAY AND LESBIAN
ALLIANCE AGAINST
DEFAMATION
150 W. 26th St., Suite 503
New York, NY 10001
(212) 807-1700
http://www.glad.org

GLOBAL CINEMA CAFE
Central Jersey Branch of
Women's International
League for Peace and
Freedom (WILPF)
Charlotte Hussey
125 Jefferson Road
Princeton, NJ 08540
(609) 497-3998

Offers free monthly video
programs addressing peace,
justice and human rights by
screening videos followed by
activist-oriented discussions
lead by community
organizers, filmmakers,
academics and experts on
the issues—all served with
coffee, tea and cookies at
the Third World Center of
Princeton University—
usually the first or second
Sunday afternoon of the
month at 4 PM.

GLOBAL EXCHANGE
2017 Mission St.
Suite 303
San Francisco, CA 94110
(415) 255-7296
Fax: (415) 255-7498
gx-info@globalexchange.org
http://www.global
    exchange.org

Publishes books and pam-
phlets on various social and
economic topics; promotes
alternative trade for the benefit of low-income producers;
helps build public awareness

about human rights abuses;
and sponsors Reality Tours to
foreign lands, giving partici-
pants a feel for the people of a
country.

GLOBALVISION
1600 Broadway, Suite 700
New York, NY 10019
(212) 246-0202
Fax: (212) 246-2677
http://www.igc.org/
    globalvision/
An independent film and television production company.
Specializing in an "inside-
out" style of journalism, it
has produced *Rights &*
Wrongs: Human Rights
Television and *South Africa*
Now along with other highly
acclaimed investigative documentaries.

GRASSROOTS NEWS
NETWORK
Pueblos Unidos building
2211 Hidalgo St.
Austin, TX 78702
(512) 441-4701
http://www.onr.com/user/
    gnnl
A non-profit, non-corporate
coalition of alternative news
and community activist
groups. The goal: to be an
alternative to the corporate
and government media which
do not serve struggles for liberty, justice, peace, or free
expression of creativity.

GREENFIRE MEDIA WATCH
Box 130 St.
Bar Harbor, ME 04609
(207) 469-2552

GREENPEACE USA
1436 U St., NW
Washington, DC 20009
(202) 462-1177
Fax: (202) 462-4507
http://www.greenpeace
    usa.org

Its purpose is to create a
green and peaceful world.
Greenpeace embraces the
principle of nonviolence,
rejecting attacks on people
and property. It allies itself
with no political party and
takes no political stance.

HELL'S KITCHEN
472 French Road
Rochester, NY 14618
(716) 234-3120
susan@hellskitchen.org

A loose coalition of groups
dedicated to cooperation and
the sharing of resources
through an AP-like setup.
It is the hope of Hell's
Kitchen that through
cooperation small groups
will gain support and that
novel "memes" will be
nurtured.

HISPANIC EDUCATION
AND MEDIA GROUP, INC.
P.O. Box 221
Sausalito, CA 94966
(415) 331-8560
Fax: (415) 331-2636
chalawerber@hotmail.com

Dedicated to improving the
quality of life of the Latino
communitywith a main focus
on high school drop-out prevention and health issues.

HUCK BOYD NATIONAL
CENTER FOR
COMMUNITY MEDIA
105 Kedzie Hall
Kansas State University
Manhattan, KS 66506
(913) 532-6890
Fax: (913) 532-5484
huckboyd@ksu.edu
http://www.jmc.ksu.edu/
    jmc/files/hbnc/hbnc.html

The mission of HBNC is to
strengthen local media in
order to help create better,
stronger communities in
America.

THE HUMANIST
MOVEMENT
197 Harbord St.
Toronto, ON M5S 1H6
Canada
(416) 535-2094
roberto@ilap.com
http://www.cynaptica.com/
    hm

Produces a wide-range of media outlets at the grassroots level through neighbourhood newspapers, neighbourhood radio and neighbourhood TV stations all over the world. These are completely non-profit, volunteer projects which focus on raising (and organizing around) issues ignored by the forces of Big Media.

HUMAN RIGHTS WATCH
350 Fifth Ave., 34th Floor
New York, NY 10118-3299
(212) 290-4700
Fax: (212) 736-1300
hrwnyc@hrw.org
http://www.hrw.org

Provides a variety of books and articles regarding worldwide human rights violations.

HUMAN RIGHTS WATCH
1522 K St., NW, Suite 910
Washington, DC 20005-1202
(202) 371-6592
Fax: (202) 371-0124
hrwdc@hrw.org
http://www.hrw.org

Exposes and works to stop human rights abuses in over 70 countries. It struggles against summary executions, torture, restrictions on the freedoms of expression, etc.

INDEPENDENT MEDIA
INSTITUTE (IMI)
Don Hazen, Exec. Director
77 Federal St.
San Francisco, CA 94107
(415) 284-1420
dhazen@igc.org
http://www.media
    democracy.org

A nonprofit organization dedicated to strengthening and supporting independent and alternative journalism, and to improving the public's access to independent information sources.

INDEPENDENT PRESS
ASSOCIATION
2390 Mission St., #201
San Francisco, CA 94110
(415) 643-4401
indypress@indypress.org
http://www.indypress.org

A membership-based association providing nuts-and-bolts technical assistance, loans, and networking to over 150 independent, progressive magazines and newspapers. Formed during the first Media & Democracy Congress in San Francisco (1996), the IPA promotes a diversity of voices on the newsstand.

INSTITUTE FOR MEDIA POLICY AND CIVIL SOCIETY
910-207 W. Hastings
Vancouver, BC V6B 1H6
Canada
(604) 682-1953
Fax: (604) 683-8536
media@impacs.bc.ca
http://www.impacs.bc.ca

Their mission is to build strong communities by providing training and education to Canadian civil society organizations.

INSTITUTE FOR POLICY STUDIES
733 15th St., NW, Suite 1020
Washington, DC 20005
(202) 234-9382
Fax: (202) 387-7915
ipsps@igc.apc.org
http://www.igc.org/ifps

Since 1963, IPS has been the nation's leading underrated progressive think tank.

INSTITUTE FOR PUBLIC ACCURACY
65 Ninth St., Suite 3
San Francisco, CA 94103
(415) 552-5378
Fax: (415) 552-6787
institute@igc.org
http://www.accuracy.org

Serves as a nationwide consortium of progressive policy researchers, scholars and activists-providing the media with quick responses to news releases from major corporate backed think tanks.

INTERNATIONAL ACTION CENTER
39 West 14th St., Rm. 206
New York, NY 10011
(212) 633-6646
Fax: (212) 633-2889
iacenter@iacenter.org
http://www.iacenter.org

Initiated in 1992 by former Attorney General Ramsey Clark and other anti-war activists, IAC coordinates international meetings, teach-ins, massive demonstrations, and publishes news releases and produces video documentaries.

INTERNATIONAL CONSORTIUM OF INVESTIGATIVE JOURNALISTS
1634 I St., NW, Suite 902
Washington, DC 20006
(202) 783-3900
Fax: (202) 783-3906
info@icij.org
http://www.icij.org

A working consortium of leading investigative reporters from around the world that sponsors investigations into pressing issues which transcend national borders.

INTERNATIONAL MEDIA
PROJECT/NATIONAL
RADIO PROJECT
1714 Franklin, #100-251
Oakland, CA 94612
(510) 251-1332
Fax: (510) 251-1342
http://www.igc.org/
  MakingContact

Produces a half-hour, weekly,
public affairs radio program
that can be heard on over 125
stations nationally, in Haiti
and South Africa, and on the
Internet as well as Radio for
Peace International. Our mission is to air the voices of
those not often heard in the
mass media.

INVESTIGATIVE
JOURNALISM PROJECT
122 Maryland Ave., NE
Suite 300
Washington, DC 20002
(202) 546-3732
Fax: (202) 543-3156

INVESTIGATIVE
REPORTING FUND
2 Wall St., Suite 203
Asheville, NC 28801-2710
(704) 259-9179
Fax: (704) 251-1311
calvina@main.nc.us
http://www.main.nc.us/fire

Keeps the heat on for the
public's right to know.

JUST THINK
FOUNDATION
80 Liberty Ship Way, Suite 1
Sausalito, CA 94965
(415) 289-0122
Fax: (415) 289-0123
think@justthink.org
http://www.justthink.org

Teaches media educators how
to integrate curriculum into
classrooms.

KLANWATCH AND
MILITIA TASKFORCE
400 Washington Ave.
Montgomery, AL 36104
(334) 264-0286
Fax: (334) 264-8891
http://www.splcenter.org.html

The Southern Poverty Law
Center created Klanwatch in
1981 in response to a resur-
gence of Ku Klux Klan activity. Today, it tracks the activities of nearly 500 organized
hate groups.

L.A. FREEWAVES
2151 Lake Shore Ave.
Los Angeles, CA 90039
(213) 664-1510
Fax: (213) 664-1577
freewaves@aol.com
http://www.freewaves.org
A multicultural media arts
network that produces festivals, workshops, curriculum
materials and a website to
encourage artistic and social
expression, serving the needs
of artists and audiences alike.

...IDE

VIDEO

...54
...co, CA 94142
...-1908
ht...//www.igc.apc.org/lvpsf/

LATINOS FOR POSITIVE
IMAGERY
160 Bennet Ave., #7A
New York, NY 10040
(212) 795-5711

LEONARD PELTIER
DEFENSE COMMITTEE
P.O. Box 583
Lawrence, KS 66044
(785) 842-5774
Fax: (785) 842-5796
lpdc@idir.net
http://members.xoom.com/
    freepeltier/index.html
http://www.freeleonard
    peltier.com

Raises awareness about
political prisoner Leonard
Peltier and current concerns
surrounding indigenous
people and prison issues.

LONG ISLAND
ALTERNATIVE MEDIA
120 Orleans Lane
Jericho, NY 11753
(516) 822-2582
robmgold@spec.net

Focuses on the production
and distribution of
progressive educational

materials. Members currently
have their own, or participate
in a number of radio and public access cable projects. A
traveling musical lecture on
Mumia Abu Jamal is currently being performed.

LOOMPANICS
UNLIMITED
P.O. Box 1197
Port Townsend, WA 98368
(360) 385-2230
Fax: (360) 385-7785
loompanix@olympus.net
http://www.loompanics.com

Champions of the First
Amendment, LU publishes
and sells publications covering a variety of controversial
topics. Has an on-line
catalogue.

LOS ANGELES
ALTERNATIVE MEDIA
NETWORK
8124 West Third St., #208
Los Angeles, CA 90048
sekler@labridge.com
Listserve: la-amn@igc.org
http://home.labridge.com/
    ~laamn/

A network of journalists in
print, radio, video and on the
Internet, dedicated to creating
a democratic media by
increasing the coverage of
those whom the media would
otherwise ignore. Through
our media outlets, we provide

a voice for the voiceless, and produce the stories which remain untold.

MEDIA ACCESS PROJECT
1707 L St., NW
Washington, DC 20036
(202) 232-4300
Fax: (202) 223-5302
http://www.mediaaccess.org/

Promotes the public's First Amendment right to hear and be heard on the electronic media. Advocates a pro-commercial model of microradio legalization.

MEDIA ALLIANCE
814 Mission St., Suite 205
San Francisco, CA 94103
(415) 546-6334
Fax: (415) 546-6218
ma@igc.org
http://www.media-alliance.org

Review and analysis of San Francisco Bay Area media isues.

THE MEDIA CHANNEL
The Media Education Project
The Global Center
(Globalvision Inc)
1600 Broadway, #700
New York, NY 10019
http://www.mediachannel.org

An online media and democracy supersite.

MEDIA COALITION/AMERICANS FOR CONSTITUTIONAL FREEDOM
139 Fulton St., Suite 302
New York, NY 10038
(212) 587-4025
Fax: (212) 587-2436
mail@mediacoalition.org
http://www.media coalition.org

Defends the American public's First Amendment right to have access to the broadest possible range of opinion and entertainment.

MEDIA CONSORTIUM, THE
2200 Wilson Blvd.
Suite 102-231
Arlington, VA 22201
(703) 920-1580
Fax: (703) 920-0946
rparry@ix.netcom.com
http://www.delve.com/ consort.html

An independent, investigative news company.

MEDIA & DEMOCRACY INSTITUTE, THE
77 Federal St.
San Francisco, CA 94107
(415) 284-1420
Fax: (415) 284-1414
congress@igc.org
http://www.alternet.org/ an/Congress.html

Dedicated to strengthening, supporting and increasing public access to independent and alternative journalism

MEDIA EDUCATION
FOUNDATION
26 Center St.
Northampton, MA 01060
(413) 586-4170
Fax: (413) 586-8398
mediaed@mediaed.org
http://www.igc.apc.org/mef/

Media research and production fostering analytical media literacy. MEF produces and distributes a number of educational videos including *The Myth of the Liberal Media* (with Noam Chomsky and Ed Herman), *Reviving Ophelia* (with Mary Pipher) and *Killing Us Softly III* (with Jean Kilbourne).

MEDIA ISLAND
INTERNATIONAL
P.O. Box 7204
Olympia, WA 98507
(360) 352 8526 voice & fax
mii@olywa.net
http://www.mediaisland.org

Works to popularize social, environmental and political justice frontline issues by helping coordinate "issues focussed" organizations with communications organizations and mapping allies for change internationally.

MEDIA NETWORK/
ALTERNATIVE MEDIA
INFORMATION CENTER
2565 Broadway, #101
New York, NY 10025
(212) 501-3841

MEDIAVISION
P.O. Box 1045
Boston, MA 02130
(617) 522-2923
Fax: (617) 522-1872
mediavi@aol.com

Works for wider exposure of progressive views through mass media. Provides stategic media consulting, training and other services for organizations and individuals.

NATIONAL ASIAN
AMERICAN
TELECOMMUNICATION
ASSOCIATION
346 9th St., 2nd Floor
San Francisco, CA 94103
(415) 863-0814
Fax: (415) 863-7428
http://www.naatanet.org

Organization seeking to increase Asian and Pacific Islanders participation in the media and the promotion of fair and accurate coverage of our communities.

NATIONAL ASSOCIATION
OF AFRICAN AMERICANS
FOR POSITIVE IMAGERY
P.O. Box 18537
Philadelphia, PA 19129
(215) 477-4133

NATIONAL ASSOCIATION
OF BLACK JOURNALISTS
8701 Adelphi Road
Adelphi, MD 20783-1716
nabj@nabj.org
http://www.nabj.org

Our mission is to strengthen
ties among African-American
journalists, promote diversity
in newsrooms, expand job
opportunities and recruiting
activities for established
African-American journalists
and students.

NATIONAL ASSOCIATION
OF HISPANIC
JOURNALISTS
National Press Bldg., Suite 1193
Washington, DC 20045
(202) 662-7145
Fax: (202) 662-7144
najh@nahj.org
http://www.nahj.org

Dedicated to the recognition
and professional advancement
of Hispanics in the news
industry.

NATIONAL ASSOCIATION
OF MINORITY MEDIA
EXECUTIVES
5746 Union Mill Rd.
Clifton, VA 20124
(703) 830-4743

NATIONAL ASSOCIATION
OF RADIO TALK SHOW
HOSTS
1030 15th St., NW, Suite 700
Washington, DC 20005
(202) 408-8255
Fax: (202) 408-5788
nashe@priority1.net
http://www.talkshow
hosts.com

Provides a resource guide to
talk radio world wide.

NATIONAL CAMPAIGN
FOR FREEDOM OF
EXPRESSION
918 F St., NW, #609
Washington, DC 20004
(202) 393-2787
Fax: (202) 347-7376
ncfe@artswire.org
http://www.artswire.org/
~ncfe/

An educational and advocacy
network of artists, arts organizations, audience members
and concerned citizens formed
to protect and extend freedom
of artistic expression and fight
censorship throughout the
United States.

NATIONAL COALITION
AGAINST CENSORSHIP
275 7th Ave., 20th Floor
New York, NY 10001
(212) 807-6222
Fax: (212) 807-6245
ncac@ncac.org
http://www.ncac.org

Works to educate members
and the public at large about
the dangers of censorship and
how to oppose it.

NATIONAL COALITION
TO PROTECT POLITICAL
FREEDOM
3321 12th St., NE
Washington, DC 20017
kgage@igc.org
www.ifconews.org/ncppf.html

National membership
organization dedicated to
protecting First Amendment
and due process rights of all
U.S. people.The NCPPF
defends the right of people
to give humanitarian and
political support to causes
in the U.S. and abroad. We
connect people under attack
with the key lawyers working
on the issues nationally,
provide legal support and
briefs; we do education and
media and strategic work
around the issues.

NATIONAL CONFERENCE
OF EDITORIAL WRITERS
6223 Executive Blvd.
Rockville, MD 20852
(301) 984-3015
Fax: (301) 231-0026
ncewhqs@erols.com
http://www.ncew.org

Dedicated to the purpose of
stimulating the conscience
and quality of the editorial.

NATIONAL EDUCATIONAL
MEDIA NETWORK
655 13th St., Suite 1
Oakland, CA 94612
(510) 465-6885
Fax: (510) 465-2835
nemn@nemn.org
http://www.nemn.org

The nation's only media
organization dedicated to
recognizing and supporting
excellence in educational
media.

NATIONAL LAWYERS
GUILD COMMITTEE
ON DEMOCRATIC
COMMUNICATIONS
558 Capp St.
San Francisco, CA 94110
(415) 522-9814
aakorn@igc.apc.org
http://www.nlgcdc.org/

Focuses on the right of all
peoples to a world-side system
of media and communications
based upon the principle of
cultural and informational

self-determination. An important force in microradio advocacy and activism.

NATIONAL LESBIAN AND GAY JOURNALISTS ASSOCIATION
1718 M St., NW, #245
Washington, DC 20036
(202) 588-9888
Fax: (202) 588-1818
nlgja@aol.com
http://www.nlgja.org

Works from within the news industry to foster fair and accurate coverage of lesbian and gay issues.

NATIONAL TELEMEDIA COUNCIL
120 East Wilson St.
Madison, WI 53703
(608) 257-7712
Fax: (608) 257-7714
Ntelemedia@aol.com
http://danenet.widip.org./ntc

A national non-profit educational organization that promotes media literacy education with a positive, non-judgmental philosophy.

NATIONAL WOMEN'S HEALTH NETWORK
1325 G St., NW
Washington, DC 20005
(202) 347-1140
Fax: (202) 347-1168

National center focusing on women's health and related issues. Publishes a bi-monthly newsletter for members.

NATIONAL WRITERS UNION
113 University Pl., 6th floor
New York, NY 10003
(212) 254-0279
Fax: (212) 254-0673
nwu@nwu.org
http://www.nwu.org/nwu/

NWU's national quarterly, *American Writer*, tracks developments in the media/information industry and the labor movement that concern working writers, and reports on union activities.

NETACTION
601 Van Ness Ave., #631
San Francisco, CA 94102
(415) 775-8674
Fax: (415) 683-3813
audrie@netaction.org
http://www.netaction.org

Educates the public, policy-makers, and media about technology policy issues; trains Internet users in how to use technology for organizing, outreach, and advocacy; promotes universal accessibility and affordability of information technology.

NEW DAY FILMS
22-D Hollywood Ave.
Ho-Ho-Kus, NJ 07423
(888) 367-9154
Fax: (201) 652-1973
orders@newday.com
http://www.newday.com

A film/video distribution
cooperative that focuses on
multiculturalism and
diversity; physical and mental
health; social and political
history; global politics; media,
art and culture; gender and
socialization; community
politics; and young adult and
family issues.

NEW MEXICO MEDIA
LITERACY PROJECT
6400 Wyoming Blvd., NE
Albuquerque, NM 87109
(505) 828-3129
Fax: (505) 828-3320
mccannon@aa.edu or
lacko@aa.edu
http://www.nmmlp.org

Their goal is to make New
Mexico the most media liter-
ate state in the U.S.

NEWSWATCH CANADA
Simon Fraser University
8888 University Dr.
Burnaby, BC V5A 1S6 Canada
(604) 291-4905
Fax: (604) 291-4024
censored@sfu.ca
http://newswatch.cprost.
sfu.ca/newswatch

Canadian media watch
organization and freedom of
information advocacy group

NEW YORK FREE
MEDIA ALLIANCE
(212) 989-8636 (info)
http://artcon.rutgers.edu/
papertiger/nyfma

A NYC-based activist group
dedicated to increasing
democracy and public space
in local and national media.
Maintains an active listserve
& website; organizes free
workshops, forums, screenings, and demonstrations.

NICAR: NATIONAL
INSTITUTE FOR
COMPUTER-ASSISTED
REPORTING
138 Neff Annex
Columbia, MO 65211
(573) 882-2042
Fax: (573) 882-5431
info@ire.org
http://www.nicar.org

NICAR trains investigative
reporters on how to use
various data bases for
investigative purposes.

NON-CONFORMING
NEWS SERVICE
Box 2505
Grass Valley, CA 95945.
(530) 477-7393
dscanlan@oro.net

A project of P.E.A.C.E.,
Inc. (Planetary Endeavor
Advocating Commitment
through Education), which
facilitates environmental,
social and economic justice
by promoting alternative
news, including the local
community access television
activists, news researchers,
and non-violence traiing
efforts.

OFFLINE
(206) 781-2044
snoegel@u.washington.edu
http://www.lightlink.com/
offline

A national arts organization
that screens cable television
and distributes independently
produced films and videos.
Serves as a creative conduit
to numerous national and
international screenings, arts
organizations, micro-cinemas,
festivals, netcast providers,
and artists.

OUR STRUGGLE/
NUESTRA LUCHA
P.O. Box 163294
Sacramento, CA 95816
(916) 361-9072
campd@csus.edu
http://www.jps.net/lryder/
index

Advocates Latino and African
American anti-racism through
various commissions and its
newsletter *Our Struggle*.

PACIFIC CENTRE FOR
ALTERNTIVE JOURNALISM
411 Thomas, N.W.
Olympia, WA 98502
(360) 754-5193
steve@intouch.bc.ca

A newly formed group that
seeks to facilitate links
between the alternative
media and organize skills and
training workshops.

PACIFIC NEWS SERVICE
450 Mission St., Room #204
San Francisco, CA 94105
(415) 438-4755; (415) 243-4364
Fax: (415) 438-4935
pacificnews@pacificnews.org
http://www.pacificnews.org/
ncm

Produces an article per day
for reprint in a variety of
newspapers worldwide.

PAPER TIGER TELEVISION
339 Lafayette St.
New York, NY 10012
(212) 420-9045
Fax: (212) 420-8223
tigertv@bway.net
http://www.papertiger.org

A non-profit volunteer
collective that has been
pioneering media criticism
through video since 1981,
conducting workshops,
creating installations and
producing videotapes. Their
programs address issues of
democratic communications,

media representation and the economics of the information industry.

THE PAUL ROBESON FUND FOR INDEPENDENT MEDIA
c/o The Funding Exchange
666 Broadway
Suite 500
New York, NY 10012
(212) 529-5300
Fax: (212) 982-9272
Viviana.Bianchi@FEX.org
http://www.fex.org/robeson

Supports media activism and grassroots organizing by local, state, national and international organizations, and individual media producers by funding radio, video and film productions.

PEOPLES VIDEO NETWORK
39 West 14th St., #206
New York, NY 10011
(212) 633-6646
Fax: (212) 633-2889
pvnnyc@peoplesvideo.org
http://www.peoplesvideo.org

A group of video activists committed to getting out news about the struggle of poor and oppressed people that the corporate media will not cover. We reach 50 cities every week plus many special editions.

PESTICIDE ACTION NETWORK
49 Powell St.
Suite 500
San Francisco, CA 94102
(415) 981-1771
Fax: (415) 981-1991
panna@panna.org
www.panna.org/panna

PIRATE TELEVISION
6057 3rd Ave. NW
Seattle, WA 98107
(206) 782-7605
edmays@scn.org

Produces a weekly public access program called "Crack the C.I.A.," which uses talks, documentaries, interviews, and rare archival news clips to expose the link between the drug trade and U.S. forign policy. The show features Gary Webb, Maxine Waters, Peter Dale Scott, Michael Levine, Noam Chomsky, Michael Ruppert, Celle Castillo, Alfred McCoy, Philip Agee, Michael Parenti, Alexander Cockburn, Jack Blum, etc.

POLITICAL RESEARCH ASSOCIATES
120 Beacon St.
Suite 202
Somerville, MA 02143-4304
(617) 661-9313
Fax: (617) 661-0059

An organization focusing on research and analysis of right wing political groups and their influence over policy making.

PROGRESSIVE MEDIA PROJECT
409 E Main St.
Madison, WI 53703
(608) 257-4626
Fax: (608) 257-3373
pmrpoj@progressive.org
http://www.progressive.org/

An affiliate of the *Progressive* magazine, edits and distributes commentaries to mainstream newspapers throughout the country.

PROJECT CENSORED
Sonoma State Univeresity
1801 E. Cotati Ave.
Rohnert Park, CA 94928
(707) 664-2500
Fax: (707) 664-2108
project.censored@sonoma.edu
http://www.sonoma.edu/
    ProjectCensored

A faculty/student media research project dedicated to building free democratic news systems. Produces an annual yearbook that discusses the year's top 25 most censored stories.

PROJECT ON GOVERNMENT OVERSIGHT
1900 L St., NW, Suite 314
Washington, DC 20036
(202) 466-5539
Fax: (202) 466-5596
pogo@pogo.org or
defense@pogo.org
http://www.pogo.org

The goal of POGO is to investigate, expose, and remedy abuses of power, mismanagement and subservience to special interests by the federal government.

PUBLIC CAMPAIGN
1320 19th St., NW
Suite M-1
Washington, DC 20036
ggomez@publicampaign.org
http://www.publicampaign.
    org.

Dedicated to sweeping reform that aims to dramatically reduce the role of special interest money in America's elections and the influence of big contributors in American politics.

PUBLIC CITIZEN
1600 20th St., NW
Washington, DC 20009
(202) 588-1000
Fax: (202) 588-7798
public_citizen@citizen.org
http://www.citizen.org

Fights for safer drugs and medical devices, cleaner and safer energy sources, a cleaner environment, fair trade, and a more open and democratic government. The consumers' eyes and ears of Washington.

PUBLIC MEDIA CENTER
446 Green St.
San Francisco, CA 94133
(415) 434-1403
Fax: (415) 986-6779

A non-profit, public interest advertising agency focusing on social, political and evironmental issues.

QUEER NEWS NETWORK
c/o C.P. Odekirk & T. Truong
Pueblos Unidos Bldg.
2211-A Hildalgo St.
Austin, Texas 78702
(512) 441-4701

A non-profit collective of gay & lesbian alternative news groups and community activist groups.

RADIO FOR ALL
http://www.radio4all.org/

The hub web site for the U.S. microradio movement, with links to clandestine stations, support groups, news and announcements, policy updates, activist alerts, legal info, and detailed primers on how to start a new station.

REPORTER'S COMMITTEE FOR FREEDOM OF THE PRESS
1101 Wilson Blvd., Suite 1910
Arlington, VA 22209
(703) 807-2100
Fax: (703) 807-2109
rcfp@rcfp.org
http://www.rcfp.org

Serves as a major national and international resource in free speech issues, disseminating information in a variety of forms, including a quarterly legal review, a bi-weekly newsletter, a 24-hour hotline, and various handbooks on media law isssues.

ROCKY MOUNTAIN MEDIA WATCH
Box 18858
Denver, CO 80218
(303) 832-7558

SATAN MACNUGGIT POPULAR ARTS
3584 John St.
Vineland Station, ON
L0R 2E0 Canada
(905) 562-7267
Fax: (905) 562-5138
looganbin@yahoo.com

An independently-run media outlet devoted to the production and distribution of radical, subversive and grassroots music, video, literature and collage art.

SEATTLE INDEPENDENT
FILM AND VIDEO
CONSORTIUM
2318 Second Ave., #313-A
Seattle, WA 98121
joel@speakeasy.org
http://www.lightlink.com/
   offline/SIFVC.html

Maintains press and public
awareness of independent
media-makers to increase dialogue between regional,
national, and international
organizations via micro-cine-
ma screenings, television,
netcasting, salon activity, art
events, its free listing service
and its world wide web
resource site.

SOCIETY OF
ENVIRONMENTAL
JOURNALISTS
P.O. Box 27280
Philadelphia, PA 19118-0280
(215) 836-9970
Fax: (215) 836-9972
SEJoffice@aol.com
http://www.sej.com/

Dedicated to supporting
environmental journalists
and furthering environmental
journalism.

SOUTHWEST
ALTERNATIVE MEDIA
PROJECT
1519 West Main St.
Houston, TX 77006
(713) 522-8592
Fax: (713) 522-0953

cyberia@swamp.org
http://www.swamp.org
A non-profit media center
promoting the creation and
appreciation of film and
video as art forms for a
multicultural public.

STRATEGY CENTER
PUBLICATIONS
Geoff Ray, Director
3780 Wilshire Blvd.
Suite 1200
Los Angeles, CA 90010
(213) 387-2800
Fax: (213) 387-3500
laborcte@igc.apc.org
http://www.igc.apc.org/
   lctr/pubmain.html

An important source for first-
hand information on direct
organizing around civil rights,
environmental racism, and
immigrant rights, with a
focuses on Los Angeles and
on transportation equity.
Many publications are bilingual English/Spanish.

TAO COMMUNICATIONS
http://www.tao.ca/

A Canada-based federation
comprised of local
autonomous collectives and
individuals. Tao organizes
networks in order to defend
and expand public space and
the right to self-determination. Host to an array of on-
line movement networks and
web sites.

TELEVISION PROJECT, THE
2311 Kimball Place
Silver Springs, MD 20910
(301) 588-4001
Fax: (301) 588-4001
apluhar@tvp.org
http://www.tvp.org

An organization to help parents understand how television affects their families and community, and propose alternatives that foster positive emotional, cognitive and spiritual development within families and communities.

THOMAS JEFFERSON CENTER FOR THE PROTECTION OF FREE EXPRESSION, THE
400 Peter Jefferson Place
Charlottesville, VA 22911
(804) 295-4784
Fax: (804) 296-3621
freespeech@tjcenter.org
http://www.tjcenter.org

An organization devoted to the defense of free expression in all its forms.

TORONTO VIDEO ACTIVIST COLLECTIVE
c/o David Hermolin
35 Manning Ave.
Toronto, ON M6J 2K3
Canada
hermolin@pathcom.com

Focused on documenting and promoting social and environmental justice

movements through taping events, organizing screenings, and conducting workshops on video activism.

TRENCH
Jeff Park
(310) 575-3500
trench1713@hotmail.com

Organizes events that investigate cross-cultural coalition building. Our founding speakers are: David Hilliard (former chief of staff, Black Panther Party), Yuri Kochiyama (Asian-American activist, personal associate of Malcolm X), Luis Rodriguez (activist, award winning author [*Always Running*], journalist and poet) and Piri Thomas (activist, poet and author of the legendary *Down These Mean St.s*).

UNION PRODUCERS AND PROGRAMMERS NETWORK
271 18th Ave. South
Minneapolis, MN 55455
(612) 624-4326
jsee@csom.umn.edu or
uppnet@labornet.org
http://www.mtn.org/jsee/
    uppnet.html

Promotes production and use of tv and radio shows pertinent to the cause of organized labor and working people—publishes UPPNET News

VANGUARD
COMMUNICATIONS
1019 19th St., N.W., Suite 1200
Washington, D.C. 20036
(202) 331-4323
Fax: (202) 331-9420
http://www.vancomm.com/

A full-service strategic communications company that
develops and implements
advocacy communications
campaigns on critical environmental, health and social
justice issues. Vanguard also
conducts media training, produces award-winning publications, stages national and
local media events, and cre-
ates innovative partnerships
for the many diverse organizations it works with.

VIDEAZIMUT
http://www.tao.ca/
    videazimut/

An international non-
governmental coalition
promoting audiovisual
communication for
development and democracy.

WE INTERRUPT THIS
MESSAGE
965 Mission St., Suite 220
San Francisco, CA 94103
(415) 537-9437
Fax: (415) 537-9439
interrupt@igc.org

Builds capacity in public
interest groups across the
country to do traditional
media work, reframe public
debate, and interrupt media
stereotypes through trainings,
technical assistance, and joint
campaigns to document and
challenge distorted news
reporting.

WHISPERED MEDIA
P.O. Box 40130
San Francisco, CA 94140
(415) 789-8484
whisper@jps.net
http://www.videoactivism.org

Provides video witnessing,
video post-production and
media resources for grassroots
activist groups. Facilitates
Bay Area Video Activist
Newtork (V.A.N.). Specializes
in direct action campaigns.

WOMEN AND MEDIA
NETWORK
http://www.ecuanex.apc.org/a
lai/wommed/ind-eng.html

Focuses on gender-balance in
access to expression and decision-making in the media,
reaffirming the importance of
fluid and pluralistic communication for women's full participation in society and promoting all forms of democratic communication.

WILD EARTH
P.O. Box 455
Richmond, VT 05477
wildearth@sprynet.com

A quarterly conservation journal that focuses on wilderness and biodiversity from an ecocentric perspective. Combining conservation biology with grassroots activism, Wild Earth is the leading source of information on wildlands protection efforts across North America.

THE WIMMIN'S ART AND TECHNOLOGY (TWAT) COLLECTIVE
731 State St.
Madison, WI 53703
(608) 262-9036

Provides a space for wimmin to share their creative abilities, work together in a collective structure, learn technical skills like construction and computer technology, and use art to create political and social change.

WOMEN FOR MUTUAL SECURITY
5110 West Penfield Road
Columbia, MD 21045
(410) 730-7483
Fax: (410) 964-9248
foerstel@aol.com
http://www.iacenter.org/wms/

A network of women's organizations and individuals committed to making a paradigm shift in the world from a heirarchical and violent mode of society to a new cooperative and peaceful model.

WOMEN'S INSTITUTE FOR FREEDOM OF THE PRESS
3306 Ross Place, NW
Washington, DC 20008-3332
(202) 966-7783
Fax: (202) 966-7783
wifponline@igc.apc.org
http://www.igc.org/wifp/

Explores ways to assure that everyone has equal access to the public, speaking for themselves, so everyone's information can be taken into account in decision-making.

WOMEN'S LEADERSHIP PROJECT
Jan Strout and
Jennifer Manlowe
1834 Old Stone Mill Dr.
Cranbury, NJ 08512
(609) 448-3819
jan.strout@fex.org or
jem45@juno.com

Organizes media literacy workshops on "Images of Women and Girls Resisting Violence" to view and discuss the images of women in media, and then create strategies to identify what helps or hinders women from preventing the violence in our lives. Workshops have been presented in many venues, from juvenile detention centers, battered women's programs, YWCA's to UN Conference on Women in Beijing.

THE WORKING GROUP
1611 Telegraph Ave.
Suite 1550
Oakland, CA 94612
(510) 268-WORK [9675]
(510) 268-3606
wedothework@igc.org

Non-profit media production
company that focuses on
ordinary, hard-working
Americans. The group has
produced the *We Do the Work*
series, the *Not In Our Town*
specials, which gained national
recognition for showcasing
positive community response
to intolerance and hate
violence. They currently
produce the award-winning
PBS series *Livelyhood*.

WORLD PRESS FREEDOM
COMMITTEE
11600 Sunrise Valley Dr.
Reston, VA 22091
(703) 715-9811
Fax: (703) 620-6790
freepress@wpfc.org

A coordination group of
national and international
news media organizations,
WPFC is an umbrella organization that includes 44 jour-
nalistic organizations united
in the defense and promotion
of freedom.

WORLDVIEWS
464 19th St.
Oakland, CA 94612-2297
(510) 451-1742
Fax: (510) 835-9631
worldviews@igc.org
http://www.igc.org/
  worldviews/

Gathers, organizes, and publi-
cizes information and educational resource materials that
deal with issues of peace and
justice in world affairs.

WORLDWATCH
INSTITUTE
1776 Massachusetts Ave., NW
Washington, DC 20036-1904
(202) 452-1999
Fax: (202) 296-7365
worldwatch@worldwatch.org
http://www.worldwatch.org/

Dedicated to fostering the
evolution of an environmentally sustainable society—
one in which human needs
are met in ways that do not
threaten the health of the
natural environment or
the prospects of future
generations.

WYMN MICRORADIO
C/O Sherri Milam
Pueblos Unidos Building
2211-A Hildalgo St.
Austin, TX 78702

Women run and built
microradio station and
collective.

THE OPEN MEDIA PAMPHLET SERIES

CORPORATE MEDIA AND THE THREAT TO DEMOCRACY
Robert W. McChesney
80 pages / $5.95 / ISBN: 1-888363-47-9

MEDIA CONTROL: THE SPECTACULAR ACHIEVEMENTS
OF PROPAGANDA Noam Chomsky
64 pages / $5.95 / ISBN: 1-888363-49-5

GENE WARS: THE POLITICS OF BIOTECHNOLOGY
Kristin Dawkins
64 pages / $4.95 / ISBN: 1-888363-48-7

GLOBALIZING CIVIL SOCIETY: RECLAIMING OUR RIGHT
TO POWER David C. Korten
80 pages / $5.95 / ISBN: 1-888363-59-2

ZAPATISTA ENCUENTRO: DOCUMENTS FROM THE 1996 ENCOUNTER
FOR HUMANITY AND AGAINST NEOLIBERALISM
The Zapatistas
64 pages / $5.95 / ISBN: 1-888363-58-4

PROPAGANDA, INC.: SELLING AMERICA'S CULTURE
TO THE WORLD Nancy Snow
80 pages / $5.95 / ISBN: 1-888363-74-6

A SUSTAINABLE ECONOMY FOR THE 21ST CENTURY
Juliet Schor
64 pages / $5.95 / ISBN: 1-888363-75-4

THE UMBRELLA OF U.S. POWER
Noam Chomsky
80 pages / $5.95 / ISBN: 1-888363-85-1

THE CASE AGAINST LAMEDUCK IMPEACHMENT
Bruce Ackerman
80 pages / $8.00 / ISBN: 1-58322-004-6

ACTS OF AGGRESSION: POLICING "ROGUE STATES"
Noam Chomsky, Edward W. Said, Ramsey Clark
64 pages / $6.95 / ISBN: 1-58322-005-4

MICRORADIO & DEMOCRACY: (LOW) POWER TO THE PEOPLE
Greg Ruggiero
64 pages / $5.95 / ISBN: 1-58322-000-3

TO ORDER ADDITIONAL SERIES TITLES CALL 1 (800) 596-7437